CIVICS 104

AMERICA'S EVOLVING BOUNDARIES

ROGER L. KEMP

authorHOUSE®

AuthorHouse™
1663 Liberty Drive
Bloomington, IN 47403
www.authorhouse.com
Phone: 833-262-8899

Published by AuthorHouse   08/18/2021

ISBN: 978-1-6655-3521-2 (sc)
ISBN: 978-1-6655-3520-5 (e)

Library of Congress Control Number: 2021916984

DEDICATION

This book is dedicated to Kieran,
The best and the brightest

ACKNOWLEDGEMENTS

Grateful acknowledgements are made to the elected officials, appointed officials, and citizens, of those cities that I have worked and lived in during my over a quarter-century public service career on both coasts of the United States.

These states and cities include the following:

- In California   –   The City of Oakland
The City of Seaside
The City of Placentia
The City of Vallejo

- In New Jersey   –   The City of Clifton

- In Connecticut   –   The City of Meriden
The Town of Berlin

CONTENTS

Lesson8: The Southern Mexico Territory Treaty

Lesson9: The Western Mexico Treaty

Lesson10: The Alaska Treaty

Lesson11: The Hawaiian Island Annexation Resolution

The Future

PREFACE

American citizens have a lot to be proud of! They live in one of the oldest democratic forms of government in the world, and this form of government in the world, and this form of government has helped create a society in which citizens are free to get involved in the political process. Citizens can vote, run for political office, endorse incumbents, promote new public office seekers, or merely back other people who do so. Also, between elections citizens are free to attend public meetings, many of which are required by law, speak about their policy and program preferences at these meetings, write letters to the editor, and even organize others to get involved in "their" political agenda.

The involvement of citizens in the American political process has changed over the years. For many years, citizens believed in *Jacksonian Democracy*, whereby they would get directly involved in the political process by attending meetings, advocating for pieces of legislation, or trying to change or invalidate legislation that they did not like. This political activism on the part of citizens primarily took place before the era of two income families, before there came to be little time for this type of political involvement. Democracy in America was founded on the principle of active political involvement on the part of its citizens.

Most adult households now have both parents working, and family time is limited to a few hours in the evenings after work. Many citizens nowadays merely elect their political representatives, and hold them accountable at voting time from election to election. This evolving type of democratic involvement on the part of citizens is called *Jeffersonian Democracy*. Many citizens have justified this type of political involvement by acknowledging that elections and voting give the common person a chance to elect the uncommon person to represent them. Under this evolving practice, the typical involvement of many citizens in the political process is merely voting at election time.

The political involvement of many Americans in years past included picketing, protesting, marching, signing petitions, attending public meetings, and publicly debating the issues. Today Americans may wear a political button, display a bumper sticker on their car, or place a candidate's sign in their front yard. Many citizens may also contribute financially to political campaigns. Because of other social and economic commitments, American citizens have evolved throughout history from engaging in very active political involvement to more passive political activities.

Everyone will agree that there is no perfect form of government, and the best form is one that has evolved and changed over time to best serve its citizens. Most citizens today take their form of government for granted. After all, it is the only form of government they have ever known. While history is provided to students in high school and college, little time is spent focusing on how our country's geographic area was established and, most importantly, how it has evolved over time to become one of the most respected national governments in the world. Many history classes start with the landing of the Pilgrims, and never cover the background and mind-set of the early settlers from the Kingdom of England. They had a form of government that greatly influenced and impacted the early settlers in the New World.

This volume focuses on how the country expanded over the years through legislation, constitutional amendments, supreme court decisions, and the impact of the evolution of our culture over time on our political processes. Many of the political changes to our democracy, and its form of government, resulted over time in response to changing citizen values and expectations. As American society evolved, so did many aspects of its democracy. These changes have manifested themselves in every changing political process, new and revised laws and regulations, as well as the magnitude and type of services provided by its governments.

For ease of reference, this volume is divided into eleven sections. This book focuses on the territorial expansion of the United States, from the establishment of the colonies to a country with fifty states. The final section examines the future of democracy, as well as its worldwide implications. Several appendices are also included to provide the reader with a greater understanding of the complex and dynamic field of America's democracy.

Territory

The nation started with the English Colony of Roanoke, which was established in 1585. This colony ceased to exist as the residents either went their own way to avoid the aboriginal people, and to find suitable farmland to grow food. The Virginia Company of Plymouth, England, was granted rights to land in what became the Colony of Virginia. The people they brought over lived in a settlement subsequently called Jamestown. The first citizens not involved in a private venture such as the Virginia Company were the Pilgrims, who landed in what later became known as the Colony of Massachusetts. The American War of Independence ultimately led to the recognition of the original 13 colonies in the New World. What was Colonial America ultimately became the United States of America, which now consists of 50 states. The documents included within relative to the territorial formation of America are listed below.

- The *Treaty of Paris*, which was approved by the Congress of the Confederation on September 3, 1783. This document led to the recognition of the original 13 colonies in the New World.
- The *Land Ordinance*, which was approved by the Congress of the Confederation on May 20, 1785. This document led to the westward expansion of the original colonies.
- The *Northwest Ordinance*, which was approved by the Congress of the Confederation on July 13, 1787, and led to the ultimate colonization of the land northwest of the Ohio River.
- The *Louisiana Purchase Treaty*, which was approved by the United States Congress on April 30, 1803. This document led to the expansion of the nation to the south and southwest of the original Thirteen Colonies.
- The *Transcontinental Treaty*, approved by the United States Congress on February 22, 1819. This document led to the expansion of the nation in parts of what would later be called the state of Florida.
- The *Resolution for the Annexation of Texas*, which was approved by the United States Congress on March 1, 1845. This document approved the voluntary annexation for the Republic of Texas to become a part of the United States of America.
- The *Oregon Treaty*, which was approved by the United States Congress on June 15, 1846. This document between the United Kingdom of Great Britain and Ireland settled the border

dispute for what was then known as Oregon Country, which is located in the northwest section of the United States.

- The *Treaty of Guadalupe Hidalgo*, which was approved by the United States Congress on February 22, 1848. This document gave the United States legal rights to southwestern and western portions of the United States.
- The *Gadsden Purchase Treaty*, which was approved by the United States Congress on December 30, 1853. This document settled the ongoing border dispute between the United States and Mexico in the territory that now forms the states of Arizona and New Mexico.
- The *Alaska Treaty*, which was approved by the United States Congress on March 30, 1867. This document approved the transfer of the Territory of Alaska from Russia to the United States of America.
- The *Hawaii Resolution*, which was approved by the United States Congress on July 7, 1898. This document approved the annexation of the Hawaiian Islands as a territory, and granted legal possession of this area to the United States of America.

The Future

The final chapter of this volume, *The Future of Democracy*, examines the impact that democracy has had on the United States of America, as well as the goal of its government to advance freedom and democracy throughout the world over the years. The author discusses the history of America's democracy, including past problems and threats, and goes on to examine international threats facing our nation and its citizens, as well as their form of government. The author states that the underlying theme of American history has been the willingness of our government, as influenced by its politicians, to defend our security and our interests in ways that, in the long run, have led to the expansion of democratic values and institutions. He concludes by stating that America, and its form of government, is looked upon as a model to emulate by citizens of other countries throughout the world. Our nation also promotes civil rights and voting rights.

Appendices

Many hours were spent researching the valuable resource materials contained in this volume. Since this volume focuses on document, every effort was made to provide background information for the reader to become more familiar with the history of America's democratic form of governance, and the various documents that have changed its boundaries over the years.

Lastly, the appendices at the end of this volume include a glossary of government terms, a history of citizen voting rights in our nation, as well as state and natural government resource directories. Closing appendices include a listing of books by the author, the world travels during his public service career, and some important "final thoughts."

Roger L. Kemp

LESSON ONE

THE ORIGINAL THIRTEEN COLONIES

Treaty of Paris

(September 3, 1783)

Congress of the Confederation

The History[1]

The American War for Independence (1775–83) was actually a world conflict, involving not only the United States and Great Britain but also France, Spain, and the Netherlands. The peace process brought a vaguely formed, newly born United States into the arena of international diplomacy, playing against the largest, most sophisticated, and most established powers on earth.

The three American negotiators, John Adams, Benjamin Franklin, and John Jay, proved themselves to be masters of the game, outmaneuvering their counterparts and clinging fiercely to the points of national interest that guaranteed a future for the United States. Two crucial provisions of the treaty were British recognition of U.S. independence and the delineation of boundaries that would allow for American western expansion.

The Treaty of Paris of 1783 ended the War of Independence and granted the thirteen colonies political freedom. A preliminary treaty between Great Britain and the United States had been signed in 1782, but the final agreement was not signed until September 3, 1783.

In the final agreement, the British recognized the independence of the United States. The treaty established generous boundaries for the United States; U.S. territory now extended from the Atlantic Ocean to the Mississippi River in the west, and from the Great Lakes and Canada in the north to the 31st parallel in the south. The U.S. fishing fleet was guaranteed access to the fisheries off the coast of Newfoundland with their plentiful supply of cod.

Navigation of the Mississippi River was to be open to both the United States and Great Britain. Creditors of both countries were not to be impeded from collecting their debts, and Congress was to recommend to the states that loyalists to the British cause during the war should be treated fairly and their rights and confiscated property restored.

The treaty is named for the city in which it was negotiated and signed. The last page bears the signatures of David Hartley, who represented Great Britain, and the three American negotiators, who signed their names in alphabetical order.

Many treaty documents, however, can be considered as originals. In this case, for example, the U.S. and British representatives signed at least three originals, two of which are in the holdings of the National Archives. On one of the signed originals the signatures and wax seals are arranged horizontally; on the other they are arranged vertically. In addition, handwritten certified copies

---

[1] Originally published as "Treaty of Paris (1783)," *100 Milestone Documents,* The National Archives, U.S. National Archives and Records Administration, College Park, Maryland, 2009. For additional information see "Treaty of Paris," *Primary Documents in American History*, Library of Congress, Washington, DC, 2009. This agency is listed in the *National Resource Directory* section of this volume.

were made for the use of Congress. Some online transcriptions of the treaty omit Delaware from the list of the former colonies, but the original text does list Delaware.

The Document

Treaty of Paris

In the name of the most holy and undivided Trinity.

It having pleased the Divine Providence to dispose the hearts of the most serene and most potent Prince George the Third, by the grace of God, king of Great Britain, France, and Ireland, defender of the faith, duke of Brunswick and Lunebourg, arch-treasurer and prince elector of the Holy Roman Empire etc., and of the United States of America, to forget all past misunderstandings and differences that have unhappily interrupted the good correspondence and friendship which they mutually wish to restore, and to establish such a beneficial and satisfactory intercourse, between the two countries upon the ground of reciprocal advantages and mutual convenience as may promote and secure to both perpetual peace and harmony; and having for this desirable end already laid the foundation of peace and reconciliation by the Provisional Articles signed at Paris on the 30th of November 1782, by the commissioners empowered on each part, which articles were agreed to be inserted in and constitute the Treaty of Peace proposed to be concluded between the Crown of Great Britain and the said United States, but which treaty was not to be concluded until terms of peace should be agreed upon between Great Britain and France and his Britannic Majesty should be ready to conclude such treaty accordingly; and the treaty between Great Britain and France having since been concluded, his Britannic Majesty and the United States of America, in order to carry into full effect the Provisional Articles above mentioned, according to the tenor thereof, have constituted and appointed, that is to say his Britannic Majesty on his part, David Hartley, Esqr., member of the Parliament of Great Britain, and the said United States on their part, John Adams, Esqr., late a commissioner of the United States of America at the court of Versailles, late delegate in Congress from the state of Massachusetts, and chief justice of the said state, and minister plenipotentiary of the said United States to their high mightinesses the States General of the United Netherlands; Benjamin Franklin, Esqr., late delegate in Congress from the state of Pennsylvania, president of the convention of the said state, and minister plenipotentiary from the United States of America at the court of Versailles; John Jay, Esqr., late president of Congress and chief justice of the state of New York, and minister plenipotentiary from the said United States at the court of Madrid; to be plenipotentiaries for the concluding and signing the present definitive treaty; who after having reciprocally communicated their respective full powers have agreed upon and confirmed the following articles.

ARTICLE 1:

His Britannic Majesty acknowledges the said United States, viz., New Hampshire, Massachusetts Bay, Rhode Island and Providence Plantations, Connecticut, New York, New Jersey, Pennsylvania, Delaware, Maryland, Virginia, North Carolina, South Carolina and Georgia, to be free sovereign and independent states, that he treats with them as such, and for himself, his heirs, and successors, relinquishes all claims to the government, propriety, and territorial rights of the same and every part thereof.

ARTICLE 2:

And that all disputes which might arise in future on the subject of the boundaries of the said United States may be prevented, it is hereby agreed and declared, that the following are and shall be their boundaries, viz.; from the northwest angle of Nova Scotia, viz., that angle which is formed by a line drawn due north from the source of St. Croix River to the highlands; along the said highlands which divide those rivers that empty themselves into the river St. Lawrence, from those which fall into the Atlantic Ocean, to the northwesternmost head of Connecticut River; thence down along the middle of that river to the forty-fifth degree of north latitude; from thence by a line due west on said latitude until it strikes the river Iroquois or Cataraquy; thence along the middle of said river into Lake Ontario; through the middle of said lake until it strikes the communication by water between that lake and Lake Erie; thence along the middle of said communication into Lake Erie, through the middle of said lake until it arrives at the water communication between that lake and Lake Huron; thence along the middle of said water communication into Lake Huron, thence through the middle of said lake to the water communication between that lake and Lake Superior; thence through Lake Superior northward of the Isles Royal and Phelipeaux to the Long Lake; thence through the middle of said Long Lake and the water communication between it and the Lake of the Woods, to the said Lake of the Woods; thence through the said lake to the most northwesternmost point thereof, and from thence on a due west course to the river Mississippi; thence by a line to be drawn along the middle of the said river Mississippi until it shall intersect the northernmost part of the thirty-first degree of north latitude, South, by a line to be drawn due east from the determination of the line last mentioned in the latitude of thirty-one degrees of the equator, to the middle of the river Apalachicola or Catahouche; thence along the middle thereof to its junction with the Flint River, thence straight to the head of Saint Mary's River; and thence down along the middle of Saint Mary's River to the Atlantic Ocean; east, by a line to be drawn along the middle of the river Saint Croix, from its mouth in the Bay of Fundy to its source, and from its source directly north to the aforesaid highlands which divide the rivers that fall into the Atlantic Ocean from those which fall into the river Saint Lawrence; comprehending all islands within twenty leagues of any part of the shores of the United States, and lying between lines to be drawn due east from the points where the aforesaid boundaries between Nova Scotia on the one part and East Florida on the other shall, respectively, touch the Bay of Fundy and the Atlantic Ocean, excepting such islands as now are or heretofore have been within the limits of the said province of Nova Scotia.

ARTICLE 3:

It is agreed that the people of the United States shall continue to enjoy unmolested the right to take fish of every kind on the Grand Bank and on all the other banks of Newfoundland, also in the Gulf of Saint Lawrence and at all other places in the sea, where the inhabitants of both countries used at any time heretofore to fish. And also that the inhabitants of the United States shall have liberty to take fish of every kind on such part of the coast of Newfoundland as British fishermen shall use, (but not to dry or cure the same on that island) and also on the coasts, bays and creeks of all other of his Britannic Majesty's dominions in America; and that the American fishermen shall have liberty to dry and cure fish in any of the unsettled bays, harbors, and creeks of Nova Scotia, Magdalen Islands, and Labrador, so long as the same shall remain unsettled, but so soon as the same or either of them shall be settled, it shall not be lawful for the said fishermen to dry or cure fish at such settlement without a previous agreement for that purpose with the inhabitants, proprietors, or possessors of the ground.

ARTICLE 4:

It is agreed that creditors on either side shall meet with no lawful impediment to the recovery of the full value in sterling money of all bona fide debts heretofore contracted.

ARTICLE 5:

It is agreed that Congress shall earnestly recommend it to the legislatures of the respective states to provide for the restitution of all estates, rights, and properties, which have been confiscated belonging to real British subjects; and also of the estates, rights, and properties of persons resident in districts in the possession on his Majesty's arms and who have not borne arms against the said United States. And that persons of any other description shall have free liberty to go to any part or parts of any of the thirteen United States and therein to remain twelve months unmolested in their endeavors to obtain the restitution of such of their estates, rights, and properties as may have been confiscated; and that Congress shall also earnestly recommend to the several states a reconsideration and revision of all acts or laws regarding the premises, so as to render the said laws or acts perfectly consistent not only with justice and equity but with that spirit of conciliation which on the return of the blessings of peace should universally prevail. And that Congress shall also earnestly recommend to the several states that the estates, rights, and properties, of such last mentioned persons shall be restored to them, they refunding to any persons who may be now in possession the bona fide price (where any has been given) which such persons may have paid on purchasing any of the said lands, rights, or properties since the confiscation.

And it is agreed that all persons who have any interest in confiscated lands, either by debts, marriage settlements, or otherwise, shall meet with no lawful impediment in the prosecution of their just rights.

ARTICLE 6:

That there shall be no future confiscations made nor any prosecutions commenced against any person or persons for, or by reason of, the part which he or they may have taken in the present war, and that no person shall on that account suffer any future loss or damage, either in his person, liberty, or property; and that those who may be in confinement on such charges at the time of the ratification of the treaty in America shall be immediately set at liberty, and the prosecutions so commenced be discontinued.

ARTICLE 7:

There shall be a firm and perpetual peace between his Britannic Majesty and the said states, and between the subjects of the one and the citizens of the other, wherefore all hostilities both by sea and land shall from henceforth cease. All prisoners on both sides shall be set at liberty, and his Britannic Majesty shall with all convenient speed, and without causing any destruction, or carrying away any Negroes or other property of the American inhabitants, withdraw all his armies, garrisons, and fleets from the said United States, and from every post, place, and harbor within the same; leaving in all fortifications, the American artilery that may be therein; and shall also order and cause all archives, records, deeds, and papers belonging to any of the said states, or their citizens, which in the course of the war may have fallen into the hands of his officers, to be forthwith restored and delivered to the proper states and persons to whom they belong.

ARTICLE 8:

The navigation of the river Mississippi, from its source to the ocean, shall forever remain free and open to the subjects of Great Britain and the citizens of the United States.

ARTICLE 9:

In case it should so happen that any place or territory belonging to Great Britain or to the United States should have been conquered by the arms of either from the other before the arrival of the said *Provisional Articles* in America, it is agreed that the same shall be restored without difficulty and without requiring any compensation.

ARTICLE 10:

The solemn ratifications of the present treaty expedited in good and due form shall be exchanged between the contracting parties in the space of six months or sooner, if possible, to be computed from the day of the signatures of the present treaty. In witness whereof we the undersigned, their ministers plenipotentiary, have in their name and in virtue of our full powers, signed with our hands the present definitive treaty and caused the seals of our arms to be affixed thereto.

Done at Paris, this third day of September in the year of our Lord, one thousand seven hundred and eighty-three.

D. HARTLEY (SEAL)
JOHN ADAMS (SEAL)
JOHN JAY (SEAL)

LESSON TWO

THE WESTERN TERRITORY ORDINANCE

Land Ordinance

(May 20, 1785)

Congress of the Confederation

The History[2]

The Land Ordinance of 1785 was adopted by the United States Congress on May 20, 1785. Under the Articles of Confederation, Congress did not have the power to raise revenue by direct taxation of the inhabitants of the United States. Therefore, the immediate goal of the ordinance was to raise money through the sale of land in the largely unmapped territory west of the original colonies acquired from Britain at the end of the Revolutionary War.

In addition, the act provided for the political organization of these territories. The earlier Ordinance of 1784 called for the land west of the Appalachian Mountains, north of the Ohio River and east of the Mississippi River to be divided into ten separate states. However, it did not define the mechanism by which the land would become states, or how the territories would be governed or settled before they became states. The Ordinance of 1785, along with the Northwest Ordinance of 1787, were intended to address these political needs.

The 1785 ordinance laid the foundations of land policy in the United States of America until passage of the Homestead Act of 1862. The Land Ordinance established the basis for the Public Land Survey System. The initial surveying was performed by Thomas Hutchins. After he died in 1789, responsibility for surveying was transferred to the Surveyor General. Land was to be systematically surveyed into square "townships," six miles (9.656 km) on a side. Each of these townships were subdivided into thirty-six "sections" of one square mile (2.59 km^2) or 640 acres. These sections could then be further subdivided for sale to settlers and land speculators.

The ordinance was also significant for establishing a mechanism for funding public education. Section 16 in each township was reserved for the maintenance of public schools. Many schools today are still located in section sixteen of their respective townships, although a great many of the school sections were sold to raise money for public education. In theory, the federal government also reserved sections 8, 11, 26 and 29 to compensate veterans of the Revolutionary War, but examination of property abstracts in Ohio indicates that this was not uniformly practiced. The Point of Beginning for the 1785 survey was where Ohio (as the easternmost part of the Northwest Territory), Pennsylvania and Virginia (now West Virginia) met, on the north shore of the Ohio River near East Liverpool, Ohio. There is a historical marker just north of the site, at the state line where Ohio Route 39 becomes Pennsylvania Route 68.

---

[2] Originally published as "Land Ordinance of 1785," *Wikipedia*, Wikipedia Foundation, Inc., San Francisco, California, November 2009. For additional information see "The New Nation, 1783–1815: Policies and Problems of the Confederated Government," *American Memory Timeline*, Library of Congress, Washington, DC, 2007. This agency is listed in the *National Resource Directory* section of this volume.

▐ The Document

Land Ordinance

An Ordinance for ascertaining the mode of disposing of Lands in the Western Territory.

Be it ordained by the United States in Congress assembled, that the territory ceded by individual States to the United States, which has been purchased of the Indian inhabitants, shall be disposed of in the following manner:

A surveyor from each state shall be appointed by Congress, or a committee of the States, who shall take an Oath for the faithful discharge of his duty, before the Geographer of the United States, who is hereby empowered and directed to administer the same; and the like oath shall be administered to each chain carrier, by the surveyor under whom he acts.

The Geographer, under whose direction the surveyors shall act, shall occasionally form such regulations for their conduct, as he shall deem necessary; and shall have authority to suspend them for misconduct in Office, and shall make report of the same to Congress or to the Committee of the States; and he shall make report in case of sickness, death, or resignation of any surveyor.

The Surveyors, as they are respectively qualified, shall proceed to divide the said territory into townships of six miles square, by lines running due north and south, and others crossing these at right angles, as near as may be, unless where the boundaries of the late Indian purchases may render the same impracticable, and then they shall depart from this rule no farther than such particular circumstances may require; and each surveyor shall be allowed and paid at the rate of two dollars for every mile, in length, he shall run, including the wages of chain carriers, markers, and every other expense attending the same.

The first line, running north and south as aforesaid, shall begin on the river Ohio, at a point that shall be found to be due north from the western termination of a line, which has been run as the southern boundary of the state of Pennsylvania; and the first line, running east and west, shall begin at the same point, and shall extend throughout the whole territory. Provided, that nothing herein shall be construed, as fixing the western boundary of the state of Pennsylvania. The geographer shall designate the townships, or fractional parts of townships, by numbers progressively from south to north; always beginning each range with number one; and the ranges shall be distinguished by their progressive numbers to the westward. The first range, extending from the Ohio to the lake Erie, being marked number one. The geographer shall personally attend to the running of the first east and west line; and shall take the latitude of the extremes of the first north and south line, and of the mouths of the principal rivers.

The lines shall be measured with a chain; shall be plainly marked by chaps on the trees and exactly described on a plat; whereon shall be noted by the surveyor, at their proper distances, all mines, salt springs, salt licks and mill seats, that shall come to his knowledge, and all water courses, mountains and other remarkable and permanent things, over and near which such lines shall pass, and also the quality of the lands.

The plats of the townships respectively, shall be marked by subdivisions into lots of one mile square, or 640 acres, in the same direction as the external lines, and numbered from 1 to 36; always beginning the succeeding range of the lots with the number next to that with which the preceding one concluded. And where, from the causes before mentioned, only a fractional part of a township shall be surveyed, the lots protracted thereon, shall bear the same numbers as if the township had been entire. And the surveyors, in running the external lines of the townships, shall, at the interval of every mile, mark corners for the lots which are adjacent, always designating the same in a different manner from those of the townships.

The geographer and surveyors shall pay the utmost attention to the variation of the magnetic needle; and shall run and note all lines by the true meridian, certifying, with every plat, what was the variation at the times of running the lines thereon noted.

As soon as seven ranges of townships, and fractional parts of townships, in the direction from south to north, shall have been surveyed, the geographer shall transmit plats thereof to the board of treasury, who shall record the same with the report, in well bound books to be kept for that purpose. And the geographer shall make similar returns, from time to time, of every seven ranges as they may be surveyed. The Secretary at War shall have recourse thereto, and shall take by lot therefrom, a number of townships, and fractional parts of townships, as well from those to be sold entire as from those to be sold in lots, as will be equal to one seventh part of the whole of such seven ranges, as nearly as may be, for the use of the late continental army; and he shall make a similar draught, from time to time, until a sufficient quantity is drawn to satisfy the same, to be applied in manner hereinafter directed. The board of treasury shall, from time to time, cause the remaining numbers, as well those to be sold entire, as those to be sold in lots, to be drawn for, in the name of the thirteen states respectively, according to the quotas in the last preceding requisition on all the states; provided, that in case more land than its proportion is allotted for sale, in any state, at any distribution, a deduction be made therefore at the next.

The board of treasury shall transmit a copy of the original plats, previously noting thereon, the townships, and fractional parts of townships, which shall have fallen to the several states, by the distribution aforesaid, to the Commissioners of the loan office of the several states, who, after giving notice of not less than two nor more than six months by causing advertisements to be posted up at the court houses, or other noted places in every county, and to be inserted in one newspaper, published in the states of their residence respectively, shall proceed to sell the townships, or fractional parts of townships, at public vendue, in the following manner, viz.: The township, or fractional part of a township, N 1, in the first range, shall be sold entire; and N 2, in the same range, by lots; and thus in alternate order through the whole of the first range. The township, or fractional part of a township, N 1, in the second range, shall be sold by lots; and N 2, in the same range, entire; and so in alternate order through the whole of the second range; and the third range shall be sold in the same manner as the first, and the fourth in the same manner as the second, and thus alternately throughout all the ranges; provided, that none of the lands, within the said territory, be sold under the price of one dollar the acre, to be paid in specie, or loan office certificates, reduced to specie value, by the scale of depreciation, or certificates of liquidated debts of the United States, including interest, besides the expense of the survey and other charges thereon, which are hereby rated at thirty six dollars the township, in specie or certificates as aforesaid, and so in the same proportion for a fractional part of a township, or of a lot, to be paid at the time of sales; on failure of which payment, the said lands shall again be offered for sale.

There shall be reserved for the United States out of every township, the four lots, being numbered 8, 11, 26, 29, and out of every fractional part of a township, so many lots of the same numbers as shall be found thereon, for future sale. There shall be reserved the lot N 16, of every township, for the maintenance of public schools, within the said township; also one third part of all gold, silver, lead and copper mines, to be sold, or otherwise disposed of as Congress shall hereafter direct.

When any township, or fractional part of a township, shall have been sold as aforesaid, and the money or certificates received therefore, the loan officer shall deliver a deed in the following terms:

The United States of America to all to whom these presents shall come, greeting:

Know ye, That for the consideration of _____ dollars we have granted, and hereby do grant and confirm _____ unto the township, (or fractional part of a township, as the case may be) numbered _____ in the range _____ excepting therefrom, and reserving one third part of all gold, silver, lead and copper mines within the same; and the lots Ns 8, 11, 26, and 29, for future sale or disposition, and the lot N 16, for the maintenance of public schools. To have to the said _____ his heirs and assigns for ever; (or if more than one purchaser to the said _____ their heirs and assigns for ever as tenants in Common.) In witness whereof, (A.B.) Commissioner of the loan office, in the State of _____ hath, in conformity to the Ordinance passed by the United States in Congress assembled, the twentieth day of May, in the year of our Lord one thousand seven hundred and eighty five, hereunto set his hand and affixed his seal this _____ day of _____ in the year of our Lord _____ and of the independence of the United States of America.

And when any township, or fractional part of a township, shall be sold by lots as aforesaid, the Commissioner of the loan office shall deliver a deed therefore in the following form:

The United States of America to all to whom these presents shall come, greeting:

Know ye, That for the consideration of _____ dollars, we have granted, and hereby do grant and confirm unto _____ the lot (or lots, as the case may be, in the township or fractional part of the township, as the case may be) numbered _____ in the range _____ excepting and reserving one third part of all gold, silver, lead and copper mines within the same, for future sale or disposition. To have to the said _____ his heirs and assigns for ever; (or if more than one purchaser, to the said _____ their heirs and assigns for ever as tenants in common). In witness whereof, (A.B.) Commissioner of the continental loan office in the state of _____ hath, in conformity to the Ordinance passed by the United States in Congress assembled, the twentieth day of May, in the year of our Lord 1785, hereunto set his hand and affixed his seal, this _____ day of _____ in the year of our Lord _____ and of the independence of the United States of America.

Which deeds shall be recorded in proper books by the commissioner of the loan office and shall be certified to have been recorded, previous to their being delivered to the purchaser, and shall be good and valid to convey the lands in the same described.

The commissioners of the loan offices respectively, shall transmit to the board of treasury every three months, an account of the townships, fractional parts of townships, and lots committed to their charge; specifying therein the names of the persons to whom sold, and the sums of money or certificates received for the same; and shall cause all certificates by them received, to be struck through with a circular punch; and they shall be duly charged in the books of the treasury, with the amount of the moneys or certificates, distinguishing the same, by them received as aforesaid.

If any township, or fractional part of a township or lot, remains unsold for eighteen months after the plat shall have been received, by the commissioners of the loan office, the same shall be returned to the board of treasury, and shall be sold in such manner as Congress may hereafter direct.

And whereas Congress by their resolutions of September 16 and 18 in the year 1776, and the 12th of August, 1780, stipulated grants of land to certain officers and soldiers of the late continental army, and by the resolution of the 22d September, 1780, stipulated grants of land to certain officers in the hospital department of the late continental army; for complying therefore with such engagements, Be it ordained, That the secretary at war, from the returns in his office, or such other evidence as the nature of the case may admit, determine who are the objects of the above resolutions and engagements, and the quantity of land to which such persons or their representatives are respectively entitled, and cause the townships, or fractional parts of townships, hereinbefore reserved for the use of the late continental army, to be drawn for in such manner as he shall deem expedient, to answer the purpose of an impartial distribution. He shall, from time to time, transmit certificates to the commissioners of the loan offices of the different states, to the lines of which the military claimants have respectively belonged, specifying the name and rank of the party, the terms of his engagement and time of his service, and the division, brigade, regiment or company to which he belonged, the quantity of land he is entitled to, and the township, or fractional part of a township, and range out of which his portion is to be taken.

The commissioners of the loan offices shall execute deeds for such undivided proportions in manner and form herein before-mentioned, varying only in such a degree as to make the same conformable to the certificate from the Secretary at War.

Where any military claimants of bounty in land shall not have belonged to the line of any particular state, similar certificates shall be sent to the board of treasury, who shall execute deeds to the parties for the same.

The Secretary at War, from the proper returns, shall transmit to the board of treasury, a certificate specifying the name and rank of the several claimants of the hospital department of the late continental army, together with the quantity of land each claimant is entitled to, and the township, or fractional part of a township, and range out of which his portion is to be taken; and thereupon the board of treasury shall proceed to execute deeds to such claimants.

The board of treasury, and the commissioners of the loan offices in the states, shall, within 18 months, return receipts to the secretary at war, for all deeds which have been delivered, as also all the original deeds which remain in their hands for want of applicants, having been first recorded; which deeds so returned, shall be preserved in the office, until the parties or their representatives require the same.

And be it further Ordained, That three townships adjacent to lake Erie be reserved, to be hereafter disposed of by Congress, for the use of the officers, men and others, refugees from Canada, and the refugees from Nova Scotia, who are or may be entitled to grants of land under resolutions of Congress now existing, or which may hereafter be made respecting them, and for such other purposes as Congress may hereafter direct. And be it further Ordained, That the towns of Gnadenhutten, Schoenbrun and Salem, on the Muskingum, and so much of the lands adjoining to the said towns, with the buildings and improvements thereon, shall be reserved for the sole use of the Christian Indians, who were formerly settled there, or the remains of that society, as may, in the judgment of the geographer, be sufficient for them to cultivate.

Saving and reserving always, to all officers and soldiers entitled to lands on the northwest side of the Ohio, by donation or bounty from the commonwealth of Virginia, and to all persons claiming under them, all rights to which they are so entitled, under the deed of cession executed by the delegates for the state of Virginia, on the first day of March, 1784, and the act of Congress accepting the same: and to the end that the said rights may be fully and effectually secured, according to the true intent and meaning of the said deed of cession and act aforesaid, Be it Ordained, that no part of the land included between the rivers called little Miami and Sciota, on the northwest side of the river Ohio, be sold, or in any manner alienated, until there shall first have been laid off and appropriated for the said Officers and Soldiers, and persons claiming under them, the lands they are entitled to, agreeably to the said deed of cession and act of Congress accepting the same.

Done by the United States in Congress assembled, the 20th day of May, in the year of our Lord 1785, and of our sovereignty and independence the ninth.

Charles Thomson, *Secretary*
Richard H. Lee, *President*

LESSON THREE

THE NORTHWEST TERRITORY ORDINANCE

Northwest Ordinance

(July 13, 1787)

Congress of the Confederation

The History[3]

The Northwest Ordinance (formally An Ordinance for the Government of the Territory of the United States, North-West of the River Ohio, and also known as the Freedom Ordinance) was an act of the Congress of the Confederation of the United States. The Ordinance unanimously passed on July 13, 1787. The primary effect of the ordinance was the creation of the Northwest Territory as the first organized territory of the United States out of the region south of the Great Lakes, north and west of the Ohio River, and east of the Mississippi River. On August 7, 1789, the U.S. Congress affirmed the Ordinance with slight modifications under the Constitution.

Arguably the single most important piece of legislation passed by members of the earlier Continental Congresses other than the Declaration of Independence, it established the precedent by which the United States would expand westward across North America by the admission of new states, rather than by the expansion of existing states.

The act also through the most empowered recognition of the importance of education and its encouragement provided for the concept of a sponsored higher education. The Morrill Act of 1862 and the Morrill Act of 1890 would follow and forever change the relationship of higher education and government. Higher education would become a tool for a good government and through the Hatch Act of 1887, an equal partner in supporting the growing needs of the expanding agrarian society.

Further, the banning of slavery in the territory had the effect of establishing the Ohio River as the boundary between free and slave territory in the region between the Appalachian Mountains and the Mississippi River. This division helped set the stage for the balancing act between free and slave states that was the basis of a critical political question in American politics in the 19th century until the Civil War.

The passage of the ordinance followed the relinquishing of all claims by the states over the territory, which was to be administered directly by Congress, with the intent of eventual admission of newly created states from the territory. The legislation was revolutionary in that it established the precedent for lands to be administered by the central government, albeit temporarily, rather than underneath the jurisdiction of particular states.

The most significant intended purpose of the legislation was its mandate for the creation of

---

[3] Originally published as "Northwest Ordinance," *Wikipedia*, Wikipedia Foundation, Inc., San Francisco, California, November 2009. For additional information see "Northwest Ordinance (1787)," *100 Milestone Documents*, U.S. National Archives and Records Administration, College Park, Maryland, 2008. This agency is listed in the *National Resource Directory* section of this volume.

new states from the region, once a population of 60,000 had been achieved within a particular territory. The actual legal mechanism of the admission of new states was established in the Enabling Act of 1802. The first state created from the territory was Ohio, in 1803.

The Northwest Ordinance, along with the Land Ordinance of 1785, laid the legal and cultural groundwork for Midwestern (and subsequently, western) development. Significantly, the free state legal philosophies of both Abraham Lincoln and Salmon P. Chase (Chief Justice, Senator, and early Ohio law author) were derived from the Northwest Ordinance.

The Document

Northwest Ordinance

An Ordinance for the government of the Territory of the United States northwest of the River Ohio.

Section 1. Be it ordained by the United States in Congress assembled, That the said territory, for the purposes of temporary government, be one district, subject, however, to be divided into two districts, as future circumstances may, in the opinion of Congress, make it expedient.

Sec. 2. Be it ordained by the authority aforesaid, That the estates, both of resident and nonresident proprietors in the said territory, dying intestate, shall descent to, and be distributed among their children, and the descendants of a deceased child, in equal parts; the descendants of a deceased child or grandchild to take the share of their deceased parent in equal parts among them: And where there shall be no children or descendants, then in equal parts to the next of kin in equal degree; and among collaterals, the children of a deceased brother or sister of the intestate shall have, in equal parts among them, their deceased parents' share; and there shall in no case be a distinction between kindred of the whole and half blood; saving, in all cases, to the widow of the intestate her third part of the real estate for life, and one third part of the personal estate; and this law relative to descents and dower, shall remain in full force until altered by the legislature of the district. And until the governor and judges shall adopt laws as hereinafter mentioned, estates in the said territory may be devised or bequeathed by wills in writing, signed and sealed by him or her in whom the estate may be (being of full age), and attested by three witnesses; and real estates may be conveyed by lease and release, or bargain and sale, signed, sealed and delivered by the person being of full age, in whom the estate may be, and attested by two witnesses, provided such wills be duly proved, and such conveyances be acknowledged, or the execution thereof duly proved, and be recorded within one year after proper magistrates, courts, and registers shall be appointed for that purpose; and personal property may be transferred by delivery; saving, however to the French and Canadian inhabitants, and other settlers of the Kaskaskies, St. Vincents and the neighboring villages who have heretofore professed themselves citizens of Virginia, their laws and customs now in force among them, relative to the descent and conveyance, of property.

Sec. 3. Be it ordained by the authority aforesaid, That there shall be appointed from time to time by Congress, a governor, whose commission shall continue in force for the term of three years, unless sooner revoked by Congress; he shall reside in the district, and have a freehold estate therein in 1,000 acres of land, while in the exercise of his office.

Sec. 4. There shall be appointed from time to time by Congress, a secretary, whose commission shall continue in force for four years unless sooner revoked; he shall reside in the district, and have a freehold estate therein in 500 acres of land, while in the exercise of his office. It shall be his duty to keep and preserve the acts and laws passed by the legislature, and the public records of the district, and the proceedings of the governor in his executive department, and transmit authentic copies of such acts and proceedings, every six months, to the Secretary of Congress: There shall also be appointed a court to consist of three judges, any two of whom to form a court, who shall have a common law jurisdiction, and reside in the district, and have each therein a freehold estate in 500 acres of land while in the exercise of their offices; and their commissions shall continue in force during good behavior.

Sec. 5. The governor and judges, or a majority of them, shall adopt and publish in the district such laws of the original States, criminal and civil, as may be necessary and best suited to the circumstances of the district, and report them to Congress from time to time: which laws shall be in force in the district until the organization of the General Assembly therein, unless disapproved of by Congress; but afterwards the Legislature shall have authority to alter them as they shall think fit.

Sec. 6. The governor, for the time being, shall be commander in chief of the militia, appoint and commission all officers in the same below the rank of general officers; all general officers shall be appointed and commissioned by Congress.

Sec. 7. Previous to the organization of the general assembly, the governor shall appoint such magistrates and other civil officers in each county or township, as he shall find necessary for the preservation of the peace and good order in the same: After the general assembly shall be organized, the powers and duties of the magistrates and other civil officers shall be regulated and defined by the said assembly; but all magistrates and other civil officers not herein otherwise directed, shall during the continuance of this temporary government, be appointed by the governor.

Sec. 8. For the prevention of crimes and injuries, the laws to be adopted or made shall have force in all parts of the district, and for the execution of process, criminal and civil, the governor shall make proper divisions thereof; and he shall proceed from time to time as circumstances may require, to lay out the parts of the district in which the Indian titles shall have been extinguished, into counties and townships, subject, however, to such alterations as may thereafter be made by the legislature.

Sec. 9. So soon as there shall be five thousand free male inhabitants of full age in the district, upon giving proof thereof to the governor, they shall receive authority, with time and place, to elect a representative from their counties or townships to represent them in the general assembly: Provided, That, for every five hundred free male inhabitants, there shall be one representative, and so on progressively with the number of free male inhabitants shall the right of representation increase, until the number of representatives shall amount to twenty five; after which, the number and proportion of representatives shall be regulated by the legislature: Provided, That no person be eligible or qualified to act as a representative unless he shall have been a citizen of one of the

United States three years, and be a resident in the district, or unless he shall have resided in the district three years; and, in either case, shall likewise hold in his own right, in fee simple, two hundred acres of land within the same; Provided, also, That a freehold in fifty acres of land in the district, having been a citizen of one of the states, and being resident in the district, or the like freehold and two years residence in the district, shall be necessary to qualify a man as an elector of a representative.

Sec. 10. The representatives thus elected, shall serve for the term of two years; and, in case of the death of a representative, or removal from office, the governor shall issue a writ to the county or township for which he was a member, to elect another in his stead, to serve for the residue of the term.

Sec. 11. The general assembly or legislature shall consist of the governor, legislative council, and a house of representatives. The Legislative Council shall consist of five members, to continue in office five years, unless sooner removed by Congress; any three of whom to be a quorum: and the members of the Council shall be nominated and appointed in the following manner, to wit: As soon as representatives shall be elected, the Governor shall appoint a time and place for them to meet together; and, when met, they shall nominate ten persons, residents in the district, and each possessed of a freehold in five hundred acres of land, and return their names to Congress; five of whom Congress shall appoint and commission to serve as aforesaid; and, whenever a vacancy shall happen in the council, by death or removal from office, the house of representatives shall nominate two persons, qualified as aforesaid, for each vacancy, and return their names to Congress; one of whom congress shall appoint and commission for the residue of the term. And every five years, four months at least before the expiration of the time of service of the members of council, the said house shall nominate ten persons, qualified as aforesaid, and return their names to Congress; five of whom Congress shall appoint and commission to serve as members of the council five years, unless sooner removed. And the governor, legislative council, and house of representatives, shall have authority to make laws in all cases, for the good government of the district, not repugnant to the principles and articles in this ordinance established and declared. And all bills, having passed by a majority in the house, and by a majority in the council, shall be referred to the governor for his assent; but no bill, or legislative act whatever, shall be of any force without his assent. The governor shall have power to convene, prorogue, and dissolve the general assembly, when, in his opinion, it shall be expedient.

Sec. 12. The governor, judges, legislative council, secretary, and such other officers as Congress shall appoint in the district, shall take an oath or affirmation of fidelity and of office; the governor before the president of congress, and all other officers before the Governor. As soon as a legislature shall be formed in the district, the council and house assembled in one room, shall have authority, by joint ballot, to elect a delegate to Congress, who shall have a seat in Congress, with a right of debating but not voting during this temporary government.

Sec. 13. And, for extending the fundamental principles of civil and religious liberty, which form the basis whereon these republics, their laws and constitutions are erected; to fix and establish those principles as the basis of all laws, constitutions, and governments, which forever hereafter shall be formed in the said territory: to provide also for the establishment of States, and permanent government therein, and for their admission to a share in the federal councils on an equal footing with the original States, at as early periods as may be consistent with the general interest:

Sec. 14. It is hereby ordained and declared by the authority aforesaid, That the following articles shall be considered as articles of compact between the original States and the people and States in the said territory and forever remain unalterable, unless by common consent, to wit:

Art. 1. No person, demeaning himself in a peaceable and orderly manner, shall ever be molested on account of his mode of worship or religious sentiments, in the said territory.

Art. 2. The inhabitants of the said territory shall always be entitled to the benefits of the writ of habeas corpus, and of the trial by jury; of a proportionate representation of the people in the legislature; and of judicial proceedings according to the course of the common law. All persons shall be bailable, unless for capital offenses, where the proof shall be evident or the presumption great. All fines shall be moderate; and no cruel or unusual punishments shall be inflicted. No man shall be deprived of his liberty or property, but by the judgment of his peers or the law of the land; and, should the public exigencies make it necessary, for the common preservation, to take any person's property, or to demand his particular services, full compensation shall be made for the same. And, in the just preservation of rights and property, it is understood and declared, that no law ought ever to be made, or have force in the said territory, that shall, in any manner whatever, interfere with or affect private contracts or engagements, *bona fide*, and without fraud, previously formed.

Art. 3. Religion, morality, and knowledge, being necessary to good government and the happiness of mankind, schools and the means of education shall forever be encouraged. The utmost good faith shall always be observed towards the Indians; their lands and property shall never be taken from them without their consent; and, in their property, rights, and liberty, they shall never be invaded or disturbed, unless in just and lawful wars authorized by Congress; but laws founded in justice and humanity, shall from time to time be made for preventing wrongs being done to them, and for preserving peace and friendship with them.

Art. 4. The said territory, and the States which may be formed therein, shall forever remain a part of this Confederacy of the United States of America, subject to the Articles of Confederation, and to such alterations therein as shall be constitutionally made; and to all the acts and ordinances of the United States in Congress assembled, conformable thereto. The inhabitants and settlers in the said territory shall be subject to pay a part of the federal debts contracted or to be contracted, and a proportional part of the expenses of government, to be apportioned on them by Congress according to the same common rule and measure by which apportionments thereof shall be made on the other States; and the taxes for paying their proportion shall be laid and levied by the authority and direction of the legislatures of the district or districts, or new States, as in the original States, within the time agreed upon by the United States in Congress assembled. The legislatures of those districts or new States, shall never interfere with the primary disposal of the soil by the United States in Congress assembled, nor with any regulations Congress may find necessary for securing the title in such soil to the bona fide purchasers. No tax shall be imposed on lands the property of the United States; and, in no case, shall nonresident proprietors be taxed higher than residents. The navigable waters leading into the Mississippi and St. Lawrence, and the carrying places between the same, shall be common highways and forever free, as well to the inhabitants of the said territory as to the citizens of the United States, and those of any other States that may be admitted into the confederacy, without any tax, impost, or duty therefor.

Art. 5. There shall be formed in the said territory, not less than three nor more than five States; and the boundaries of the States, as soon as Virginia shall alter her act of cession, and consent to the same, shall become fixed and established as follows, to wit: The western State in the said territory, shall be bounded by the Mississippi, the Ohio, and Wabash Rivers; a direct line drawn from the Wabash and Post Vincents, due North, to the territorial line between the United States and Canada; and, by the said territorial line, to the Lake of the Woods and Mississippi. The middle State shall be bounded by the said direct line, the Wabash from Post Vincents to the Ohio, by the Ohio, by a direct line, drawn due north from the mouth of the Great Miami, to the said territorial line, and by the said territorial line. The eastern State shall be bounded by the last mentioned direct line, the Ohio, Pennsylvania, and the said territorial line: *Provided, however*, and it is further understood and declared, that the boundaries of these three States shall be subject so far to be altered, that, if Congress shall hereafter find it expedient, they shall have authority to form one or two States in that part of the said territory which lies north of an east and west line drawn through the southerly bend or extreme of Lake Michigan. And, whenever any of the said States shall have sixty thousand free inhabitants therein, such State shall be admitted, by its delegates, into the Congress of the United States, on an equal footing with the original States in all respects whatever, and shall be at liberty to form a permanent constitution and State government: Provided, the constitution and government so to be formed, shall be republican, and in conformity to the principles contained in these articles; and, so far as it can be consistent with the general interest of the confederacy, such admission shall be allowed at an earlier period, and when there may be a less number of free inhabitants in the State than sixty thousand.

Art. 6. There shall be neither slavery nor involuntary servitude in the said territory, otherwise than in the punishment of crimes whereof the party shall have been duly convicted: Provided, always, That any person escaping into the same, from whom labor or service is lawfully claimed in any one of the original States, such fugitive may be lawfully reclaimed and conveyed to the person claiming his or her labor or service as aforesaid.

Be it ordained by the authority aforesaid, That the resolutions of the 23rd of April, 1784, relative to the subject of this ordinance, be, and the same are hereby repealed and declared null and void.

Done by the United States, in Congress assembled, the 13th day of July, in the year of our Lord 1787, and of their sovereignty and independence the twelfth.

LESSON FOUR

THE FRENCH TERRITORY TREATY

Louisiana Purchase Treaty

(April 30, 1803)

United States Congress

The History[4]

The story of the way in which the United States acquired Louisiana is complicated, involving power, politics, intrigue, and suspicion. It also reveals the foresight of Thomas Jefferson, who considered the purchase as one of his greatest achievements.

At the end of the French and Indian Wars in 1763, France lost all of its possessions in North America, dashing hopes of a colonial empire. This empire was centered on the Caribbean island of Santo Domingo and its lucrative cash crop of sugar. The French territory called Louisiana, extending from New Orleans up the Missouri River to modern-day Montana, was intended as a granary for this empire and produced flour, salt, lumber, and food for the sugar islands. By the terms of the 1763 Treaty of Fontainbleau, however, Louisiana west of the Mississippi was ceded to Spain, while the victorious British received the eastern portion of the huge colony.

When the United States won its independence from Great Britain in 1783, one of its major concerns was having a European power on its western boundary, and the need for unrestricted access to the Mississippi River. As American settlers pushed west, they found that the Appalachian Mountains provided a barrier to shipping goods eastward. The easiest way to ship produce was to build a flatboat and float down the Ohio and Mississippi Rivers to the port of New Orleans, from which goods could be put on ocean-going vessels. The problem with this route was that the Spanish owned both sides of the Mississippi below Natchez.

In 1795 the United States negotiated the Pinckney Treaty with Spain, which provided the right of navigation on the river and the right of deposit of U.S. goods at the port of New Orleans. The treaty was to remain in effect for three years, with the possibility of renewal. By 1802, U.S. farmers, businessmen, trappers and lumbermen were bringing over $1 million worth of produce through New Orleans each year. Spanish officials were becoming concerned, as U.S. settlement moved closer to their territory. Spain was eager to divest itself of Louisiana, which was a drain on its financial resources. On October 1, 1800, Napoleon Bonaparte, First Consul of France, concluded the Treaty of San Ildefonso with Spain, which returned Louisiana to French ownership in exchange for a Spanish kingdom in Italy. Napoleon's ambitions in Louisiana involved the creation of a new empire centered on the Caribbean sugar trade. By terms of the Treaty of Ameins of 1800, Great Britain returned ownership of the islands of Martinique and Guadaloupe to the

---

[4] Originally published as "The United States Takes Posession of the Louisiana Territory," *The Journey of Discovery*, National Park Service, U.S. Department of the Interior, Washington, DC, May 2007. For additional information see "Louisiana Purchase," *The Lewis and Clark Journey of Discovery*, Nation Park Service, U.S. Department of the Interior, Washington, DC, 2008. This agency is listed in the *National Resource Directory* section of this volume.

French. Napoleon looked upon Louisiana as a depot for these sugar islands, and as a buffer to U.S. settlement. In October of 1801 he sent a large military force to retake the important island of Santa Domingo, lost in a slave revolt in the 1790s.

Thomas Jefferson, third President of the United States, was disturbed by Napoleon's plans to re-establish French colonies in America. With the possession of New Orleans, Napoleon could close the Mississippi to U.S. commerce at any time. Jefferson authorized Robert R. Livingston, U.S. Minister to France, to negotiate for the purchase for up to $2 million of the City of New Orleans, portions of the east bank of the Mississippi, and free navigation of the river for U.S. commerce.

An official transfer of Louisiana to French ownership had not yet taken place, and Napoleon's deal with the Spanish was a poorly kept secret of the frontier. On October 18, 1802, however, a strange thing happened. Juan Ventura Moralis, Acting Intendant of Louisiana, made public the intention of Spain to revoke the right of deposit at New Orleans for all cargo from the United States. The closure of this vital port to the United States caused anger and consternation, and commerce in the west was virtually blockaded. Historians believe that the revocation of the right of deposit was prompted by abuses of the Americans, particularly smuggling, and not by French intrigues as was believed at the time. President Jefferson ignored public pressure for war with France, and appointed James Monroe special envoy to Napoleon, to assist in obtaining New Orleans for the United States. Jefferson boosted the authorized expenditure of funds to $10 million.

Meanwhile, Napoleon's plans in the Caribbean were being frustrated by Toussaint L'Ouverture, his army of former slaves, and yellow fever. During ten months of fierce fighting on Santo Domingo, France lost more than 40,000 soldiers. Without Santo Domingo Napoleon's colonial ambitions for a French empire were foiled in North America. Louisiana would be useless as a granary without sugar islanders to feed. Napoleon also considered the temper of the United States, where sentiment was growing against France and strong ties with Great Britain were being considered. Spain's refusal to sell Florida was the last straw, and Napoleon turned his attention once more to Europe; the sale of the now-useless Louisiana would supply needed funds to wage war there. Napoleon directed his ministers, Talleyrand and Barbé-Marbois, to offer the entire Louisiana territory to the United States —— and quickly.

On April 11, 1803, Talleyrand asked Robert Livingston how much the United States was prepared to pay for Louisiana. Livingston was confused, as his instructions only covered the purchase of New Orleans and the immediate area, not the entire Louisiana territory. James Monroe agreed with Livingston that Napoleon might withdraw this offer at any time. To wait for approval from President Jefferson might take months, so Livingston and Monroe decided to open negotiations immediately. By April 30, they closed a deal for the purchase of the entire 828,000 square mile Louisiana territory for 60 million Francs (approximately $15 million). Part of this sum was used to forgive debts owed by France to the United States. The payment was made in United States bonds, which Napoleon sold at face value to the Dutch firm of Hope and Company, and the British banking house of Baring, at a discount of 87½ per each $100 unit. As a result, Napoleon received only $8,831,250 in cash for Louisiana. Dutiful banker Alexander

Baring conferred with Marbois in Paris, shuttled to the United States to pick up the bonds, took them to Britain, and returned to France with the money — and Napoleon used these funds to wage war against Baring's own country!

When news of the purchase reached the United States, President Jefferson was surprised. He had authorized the expenditure of $10 million for a port city, and instead received treaties committing the government to spend $15 million on a land package which would double the size of the country. Jefferson's political opponents in the Federalist Party argued that the Louisiana purchase was a worthless desert, and that the Constitution did not provide for the acquisition of new land or negotiating treaties without the consent of the Senate. What really worried the opposition was the new states which would inevitably be carved from the Louisiana territory, strengthening Western and Southern interests in Congress, and further reducing the influence of New England Federalists in national affairs. President Jefferson was an enthusiastic supporter of westward expansion, and held firm in his support for the treaty. Despite Federalist objections, the U.S. Senate ratified the Louisiana treaty in the autumn of 1803.

A transfer ceremony was held in New Orleans on November 29, 1803. Since the Louisiana territory had never officially been turned over to the French, the Spanish took down their flag, and the French raised theirs. The following day, General James Wilkinson accepted possession of New Orleans for the United States. A similar ceremony was held in St. Louis on March 9, 1804, when a French tricolor was raised near the river, replacing the Spanish national flag. The following day, Captain Amos Stoddard of the First U.S. Artillery marched his troops into town and ran the stars and stripes up the fort's flagpole. The Louisiana territory was officially transferred to the United States government, represented by Meriwether Lewis.

The Louisiana Territory, purchased for less than 5 cents an acre, was one of Thomas Jefferson's greatest contributions to his country. Louisiana doubled the size of the United States literally overnight, without a war or the loss of a single American life, and set a precedent for the purchase of territory. It opened the way for the eventual expansion of the United States across the continent to the Pacific, and its consequent rise to the status of world power. International affairs in the Caribbean and Napoleon's hunger for cash to support his war efforts were the background for a glorious achievement of Thomas Jefferson's presidency, new lands, and new opportunities for the nation.

The Document

Louisiana Purchase Treaty

TREATY BETWEEN THE UNITED STATES OF AMERICA AND THE FRENCH REPUBLIC

The President of the United States of America and the First Consul of the French Republic in the name of the French People desiring to remove all Source of misunderstanding relative to objects of discussion mentioned in the Second and fifth articles of the Convention of the 8th Vendémiaire on 9/30 September 1800 relative to the rights claimed by the United States in virtue of the Treaty concluded at Madrid the 27 of October 1795, between His Catholic Majesty & the Said United States, & willing to Strengthen the union and friendship which at the time of the Said Convention was happily reestablished between the two nations have respectively named their Plenipotentiaries to wit The President of the United States, by and with the advice and consent of the Senate of the Said States; Robert R. Livingston Minister Plenipotentiary of the United States and James Monroe Minister Plenipotentiary and Envoy extraordinary of the Said States near the Government of the French Republic; And the First Consul in the name of the French people, Citizen Francis Barbé Marbois Minister of the public treasury who after having respectively exchanged their full powers have agreed to the following Articles.

Article I

Whereas by the Article the third of the Treaty concluded at St. Ildefonso the 9th Vendémiaire on 1st October 1800 between the First Consul of the French Republic and his Catholic Majesty it was agreed as follows.

"His Catholic Majesty promises and engages on his part to cede to the French Republic six months after the full and entire execution of the conditions and Stipulations herein relative to his Royal Highness the Duke of Parma, the Colony or Province of Louisiana with the Same extent that it now has in the hand of Spain, & that it had when France possessed it; and Such as it Should be after the Treaties subsequently entered into between Spain and other States."

And whereas in pursuance of the Treaty and particularly of the third article the French Republic has an incontestible title to the domain and to the possession of the said Territory –– The First Consul of the French Republic desiring to give to the United States a strong proof of his friendship doth hereby cede to the United States in the name of the French Republic for ever and in full Sovereignty the said territory with all its rights and appurtenances as fully and in the Same manner as they have been acquired by the French Republic in virtue of the above mentioned Treaty concluded with his Catholic Majesty.

Art: II

In the cession made by the preceeding article are included the adjacent Islands belonging to Louisiana all public lots and Squares, vacant lands and all public buildings, fortifications, barracks and other edifices which are not private property. –– The Archives, papers & documents relative to the domain and Sovereignty of Louisiana and its dependances will be left in the possession of the Commissaries of the United States, and copies will be afterwards given in due form to the Magistrates and Municipal officers of such of the said papers and documents as may be necessary to them.

Art: III

The inhabitants of the ceded territory shall be incorporated in the Union of the United States and admitted as soon as possible according to the principles of the federal Constitution to the enjoyment of all these rights, advantages and immunities of citizens of the United States, and in the mean time they shall be maintained and protected in the free enjoyment of their liberty, property and the Religion which they profess.

Art: IV

There Shall be Sent by the Government of France a Commissary to Louisiana to the end that he do every act necessary as well to receive from the Officers of his Catholic Majesty the Said country and its dependances in the name of the French Republic if it has not been already done as to transmit it in the name of the French Republic to the Commissary or agent of the United States.

Art: V

Immediately after the ratification of the present Treaty by the President of the United States and in case that of the first Consul's shall have been previously obtained, the commissary of the French Republic shall remit all military posts of New Orleans and other parts of the ceded territory to the Commissary or Commissaries named by the President to take possession – the troops whether of France or Spain who may be there shall cease to occupy any military post from the time of taking possession and shall be embarked as soon as possible in the course of three months after the ratification of this treaty.

Art: VI

The United States promise to execute Such treaties and articles as may have been agreed between Spain and the tribes and nations of Indians until by mutual consent of the United States and the said tribes or nations other Suitable articles Shall have been agreed upon.

Art: VII

As it is reciprocally advantageous to the commerce of France and the United States to encourage the communication of both nations for a limited time in the country ceded by the present treaty until general arrangements relative to commerce of both nations may be agreed on; it has been agreed between the contracting parties that the French Ships coming directly from France or any of her colonies loaded only with the produce and manufactures of France or her Said Colonies; and the Ships of Spain coming directly from Spain or any of her colonies loaded only with the produce or manufactures of Spain or her Colonies shall be admitted during the Space of twelve years in the Port of New-Orleans and in all other legal ports-of-entry within the ceded territory in the Same manner as the Ships of the United States coming directly from France or Spain or any of their Colonies without being Subject to any other or greater duty on merchandize or other or greater tonnage than that paid by the citizens of the United States.

During that Space of time above mentioned no other nation Shall have a right to the Same privileges in the Ports of the ceded territory –– the twelve years Shall commence three months after the exchange of ratifications if it Shall take place in France or three months after it Shall have been notified at Paris to the French Government if it Shall take place in the United States; It is however well understood that the object of the above article is to favour the manufactures, Commerce, freight and navigation of France and of Spain So far as relates to the importations that the French and Spanish Shall make into the Said Ports of the United States without in any Sort affecting the regulations that the United States may make concerning the exportation of the produce and merchandize of the United States, or any right they may have to make Such regulations.

Art: VIII

In future and for ever after the expiration of the twelve years, the Ships of France shall be treated upon the footing of the most favoured nations in the ports above mentioned.

Art: IX

The particular Convention Signed this day by the respective Ministers, having for its object to provide for the payment of debts due to the Citizens of the United States by the French Republic prior to the 30th Sept. 1800 (8th Vendémiaire an 9) is approved and to have its execution in the Same manner as if it had been inserted in this present treaty, and it Shall be ratified in the same form and in the Same time So that the one Shall not be ratified distinct from the other.

Another particular Convention Signed at the Same date as the present treaty relative to a definitive rule between the contracting parties is in the like manner approved and will be ratified in the Same form, and in the Same time and jointly.

Art: X

The present treaty Shall be ratified in good and due form and the ratifications Shall be exchanged in the Space of Six months after the date of the Signature by the Ministers Plenipotentiary or Sooner if possible.

In faith whereof the respective Plenipotentiaries have Signed these articles in the French and English languages; declaring nevertheless that the present Treaty was originally agreed to in the French language; and have thereunto affixed their Seals.

Done at Paris the tenth day of Floreal in the eleventh year of the French Republic; and the 30th of April 1803.

    Robt R Livingston [seal]
    Jas. Monroe [seal]
    Barbé Marbois [seal]

The *Louisiana Purchase Treaty* of April 30, 1803, between the United States of America and the French Republic (as outlined above), was accompanied by two (2) convention agreements to pay for this historical land acquisition. The first convention agreement was for the payment of

60 million francs ($11,250,000), and the other was made for claims that American citizens had made against France in the amount of 20 million francs ($3,750,000).

While the primary land acquisition treaty is outlined above, the two (2) convention agreements necessary to implement this treaty are transcribed below. Both of these other agreements, also dated April 30, 1803, were essential to the implementation of the Louisiana Purchase Treaty.

A CONVENTION BETWEEN THE UNITED STATES OF AMERICA AND THE FRENCH REPUBLIC

The President of the United States of America and the First Consul of the French Republic in the name of the French people, in consequence of the treaty of cession of Louisiana which has been Signed this day; wishing to regulate definitively every thing which has relation to the Said cession have authorized to this effect the Plenipotentiaries, that is to say the President of the United States has, by and with the advice and consent of the Senate of the Said States, nominated for their Plenipotentiaries, Robert R. Livingston, Minister Plenipotentiary of the United States, and James Monroe, Minister Plenipotentiary and Envoy-Extraordinary of the Said United States, near the Government of the French Republic; and the First Consul of the French Republic, in the name of the French people, has named as Plenipotentiary of the Said Republic the citizen Francis Barbé Marbois who, in virtue of their full powers, which have been exchanged this day, have agreed to the followings articles:

Art: 1

The Government of the United States engages to pay to the French government in the manner Specified in the following article the sum of Sixty millions of francs independant of the Sum which Shall be fixed by another Convention for the payment of the debts due by France to citizens of the United States.

Art: 2

For the payment of the Sum of Sixty millions of francs mentioned in the preceeding article the United States shall create a Stock of eleven millions, two hundred and fifty thousand Dollars bearing an interest of Six per cent: per annum payable half yearly in London Amsterdam or Paris amounting by the half year to three hundred and thirty Seven thousand five hundred Dollars, according to the proportions which Shall be determined by the french Government to be paid at either place: The principal of the Said Stock to be reimbursed at the treasury of the United States in annual payments of not less than three millions of Dollars each; of which the first payment Shall commence fifteen years after the date of the exchange of ratifications: —— this Stock Shall be transferred to the government of France or to Such person or persons as Shall be authorized to receive it in three months at most after the exchange of ratifications of this treaty and after Louisiana Shall be taken possession of the name of the Government of the United States.

It is further agreed that if the french Government Should be desirous of disposing of the Said Stock to receive the capital in Europe at Shorter terms that its measures for that purpose Shall be taken So as to favour in the greatest degree possible the credit of the United States, and to raise to the highest price the Said Stock.

Art: 3

It is agreed that the Dollar of the United States Specified in the present Convention shall be fixed at five francs 3333/100000 or five livres eight Sous tournois.

The present Convention Shall be ratified in good and due form, and the ratifications Shall be exchanged the Space of Six months to date from this day or Sooner it possible.

In faith of which the respective Plenipotentiaries have Signed the above articles both in the french and english languages, declaring nevertheless that the present treaty has been originally agreed on and written in the french language; to which they have hereunto affixed their Seals.

Done at Paris the tenth of Floreal eleventh year of the french Republic.

30ᵗʰ April 1803.

> Robt R Livingston [seal]
> Jas. Monroe [seal]
> Barbé Marbois [seal]

Convention between the United States of America and the French Republic

The President of the United States of America and the First Consul of the French Republic in the name of the French People having by a Treaty of this date terminated all difficulties relative to Louisiana, and established on a Solid foundation the friendship which unites the two nations and being desirous in complyance with the Second and fifth Articles of the Convention of the 8ᵗʰ Vendémiaire ninth year of the French Republic (30ᵗʰ September 1800) to Secure the payment of the Sums due by France to the citizens of the United States have respectively nominated as Plenipotentiaries that is to Say The President of the United States of America by and with the advise and consent of their Senate Robert R. Livingston Minister Plenipotentiary and James Monroe Minister Plenipotentiary and Envoy Extraordinary of the Said States near the Government of the French Republic: and the First Consul in the name of the French People the Citizen Francis Barbé Marbois Minister of the public treasury; who after having exchanged their full powers have agreed to the following articles.

Art: 1

The debts due by France to citizens of the United States contracted before the 8ᵗʰ Vendémiaire ninth year of the French Republic (30ᵗʰ September 1800) shall be paid according to the following regulations with interest at Six per Cent; to commence from the period when the accounts and vouchers were presented to the French Government.

Art: 2

The debts provided for by the preceeding Article are those whose result is comprised in the conjectural note annexed to the present Convention and which, with the interest cannot exceed the Sum of twenty millions of Francs. The claims comprised in the Said note which fall within the exceptions of the following articles, Shall not be admitted to the benefit of this provision.

Art: 3

The principal and interests of the Said debts Shall be discharged by the United States, by orders drawn by their Minister Plenipotentiary on their treasury, these orders Shall be payable Sixty days after the exchange of ratifications of the Treaty and the Conventions Signed this day, and after possession Shall be given of Louisiana by the Commissaries of France to those of the United States.

Art: 4

It is expressly agreed that the preceding articles Shall comprehend no debts but Such as are due to citizens of the United States who have been and are yet creditors of France for Supplies for embargoes and prizes made at Sea, in which the appeal has been properly lodged within the time mentioned in the Said Convention 8th Vendémiaire ninth year, (30th Sept 1800).

Art: 5

The preceding Articles Shall apply only, First: to captures of which the council of prizes Shall have ordered restitution, it being well understood that the claimant cannot have recourse to the United States otherwise than he might have had to the Government of the French republic, and only in case of insufficiency of the captors —— 2d the debts mentioned in the Said fifth Article of the Convention contracted before the 8th Vendémiaire an 9/30th September 1800 the payment of which has been heretofore claimed of the actual Government of France and for which the creditors have a right to the protection of the United States; —— the Said 5th Article does not comprehend prizes whose condemnation has been or Shall be confirmed: it is the express intention of the contracting parties not to extend the benefit of the present Convention to reclamations of American citizens who Shall have established houses of Commerce in France, England or other countries than the United States in partnership with foreigners, and who by that reason and the nature of their commerce ought to be regarded as domiciliated in the places where Such house exist. —— All agreements and bargains concerning merchandize, which Shall not be the property of American citizens, are equally excepted from the benefit of the said Conventions, Saving however to Such persons their claims in like manner as if this Treaty had not been made.

Art: 6

And that the different questions which may arise under the preceding article may be fairly investigated, the Ministers Plenipotentiary of the United States Shall name three persons, who Shall act from the present and provisionally, and who shall have full power to examine, without removing the documents, all the accounts of the different claims already liquidated by the Bureaus established for this purpose by the French Republic, and to ascertain whether they belong to the classes designated by the present Convention and the principles established in it or if they are not in one of its exceptions and on their Certificate, declaring that the debt is due to an American Citizen or his representative and that it existed before the 8th Vendémiaire 9th year/30 September 1800 the debtor shall be entitled to an order on the Treasury of the United States in the manner prescribed by the 3d Article.

Art: 7

The Same agents Shall likewise have power, without removing the documents, to examine the claims which are prepared for verification, and to certify those which ought to be admitted by uniting the necessary qualifications, and not being comprised in the exceptions contained in the present Convention.

Art: 8

The Same agents shall likewise examine the claims which are not prepared for liquidation, and certify in writing those which in their judgement ought to be admitted to liquidation.

Art: 9

In proportion as the debts mentioned in these articles Shall be admitted they Shall be discharged with interest at Six per Cent: by the Treasury of the United States.

Art: 10

And that no debt shall not have the qualifications above mentioned and that no unjust or exorbitant demand may be admitted, the Commercial agent of the United States at Paris or such other agent as the Minister Plenipotentiary or the United States Shall think proper to nominate shall assist at the operations of the Bureaus and cooperate in the examinations of the claims; and if this agent Shall be of the opinion that any debt is not completely proved, or if he shall judge that it is not comprised in the principles of the fifth article above mentioned, and if notwithstanding his opinion the Bureaus established by the french Government should think that it ought to be liquidated, he shall transmit his observations to the board established by the United States, who, without removing documents, shall make a complete examination of the debt and vouchers which Support it, and report the result to the Minister of the United States. –– The Minister of the

United States Shall transmit his observations in all Such cases to the Minister of the treasury of the French Republic, on whose report the French Government Shall decide definitively in every case.

The rejection of any claim Shall have no other effect than to exempt the United States from the payment of it, the French Government reserving to itself, the right to decide definitively on Such claim So far as it concerns itself.

Art: 11

Every necessary decision Shall be made in the course of a year to commence from the exchange of ratifications, and no reclamation Shall be admitted afterwards.

Art: 12

In case of claims for debts contracted by the Government of France with citizens of the United States Since the 8th Vendémiaire 9th year/30 September 1800 not being comprised in this Convention may be pursued, and the payment demanded in the Same manner as if it had not been made.

Art: 13

The present convention Shall be ratified in good and due form and the ratifications Shall be exchanged in Six months from the date of the Signature of the Ministers Plenipotentiary, or Sooner if possible.

In faith of which, the respective Ministers Plenipotentiary have signed the above Articles both in the french and english languages, declaring nevertheless that the present treaty has been originally agreed on and written in the french language, to which they have hereunto affixed their Seals.

Done at Paris, the tenth of Floreal, eleventh year of the French Republic.

30th April 1803.

Robt R Livingston [seal]

Jas. Monroe [seal]

Barbé Marbois [seal]

LESSON FIVE

THE WEST FLORIDA TERRITORY TREATY

Transcontinental Treaty

(February 22, 1819)

United States Congress

The History[5]

The colonies of East Florida and West Florida remained loyal to the British during the war for American Independence, but by the Treaty of Paris in 1783 they returned to Spanish control. After 1783, American immigrants moved into West Florida. In 1810, these American settlers in West Florida rebelled, declaring independence from Spain. President James Madison and Congress used the incident to claim the region, knowing full well that the Spanish government was seriously weakened by Napoleon's invasion of Spain.

The United States asserted that the portion of West Florida from the Mississippi to the Peridido rivers was part of the Louisiana Purchase of 1803. Negotiations over Florida began in earnest with the mission of Don Luis de Onís to Washington in 1815 to meet Secretary of State James Monroe. The issue was not resolved until Monroe was president and John Quincy Adams his Secretary of State.

Although U.S.–Spanish relations were strained over suspicions of American support for the independence struggles of Spanish-American colonies, the situation became critical when General Andrew Jackson seized the Spanish forts at Pensacola and St. Marks in his 1818 authorized raid against Seminoles and escaped slaves who were viewed as a threat to Georgia. Jackson executed two British citizens on charges of inciting the Indians and runaways.

Monroe's government seriously considered denouncing Jackson's actions, but Adams defended Jackson citing the necessity to restrain the Indians and escaped slaves since the Spanish failed to do so. Adams also sensed that Jackson's Seminole campaign was popular with Americans and it strengthened his diplomatic hand with Spain.

Adam used Jackson's military action to present Spain with a demand to either control the inhabitants of East Florida or cede it to the United States. Minister Onís and Secretary Adams reached an agreement whereby Spain ceded East Florida to the United States and renounced all claim to West Florida. Spain received no compensation, but the United States agreed to assume liability for $5 million in damage done by American citizens who rebelled against Spain.

Under the Onís-Adams Treaty of 1819 (also called the Transcontinental Treaty and ratified

---

[5] Originally published as "Acquisition of Florida: Treaty of Adams-Onis (1819) and Transcontinental Treaty (1821)," *Timeline of U.S. Diplomatic History (1801–1829)*, Office of the Historian, Bureau of Public Affairs, U.S. Department of State, Washington, DC, 2000. For additional information see "Acquisition of Florida: Treaty of Adams-Onis (1819) and Transcontinental Treaty (1821)," *Timeline of U.S. Diplomatic History (1801–1829)*, Office of the Historian, Bureau of Public Affairs, U.S. Department of State, Washington, DC, 2004. This agency is listed in the *National Resource Directory* section of this volume.

in 1821) the United States and Spain defined the western limits of the Louisiana Purchase and Spain surrendered its claims to the Pacific Northwest. In return, the United States recognized Spanish sovereignty over Texas.

The Document

Transcontinental Treaty

The United States of America and His Catholic Majesty, desiring to consolidate, on a permanent basis, the friendship and good correspondence which happily prevails between the two parties, have determined to settle and terminate all their differences and pretensions, by a treaty, which shall designate, with precision, the limits of their respective bordering territories in North America.

With this intention the President of the United States has furnished with their full powers John Quincy Adams, Secretary of State of the said United States; and His Catholic Majesty has appointed the Most Excellent Lord Don Luis De On's, Gonzales, Lopez y Vara, Lord of the Town of Rayaces, Perpetual Regidor of the Corporation of the city of Salamanca, Knight Grand Cross of the Royal American Order of Isabella the Catholic, decorated with the Lys of La Vendee, Knight Pensioner of the Royal and Distinguished Spanish Order of Charles the Third, Member of the Supreme Assembly of the said Royal Order; of the Council of His Catholic Majesty; his Secretary, with Exercise of Decrees, and His Envoy Extraordinary and Minister Plenipotentiary near the United States of America.

And the said Plenipotentiaries, after having exchanged their powers, have agreed upon and concluded the following articles:

ARTICLE I

There shall be a firm and inviolable peace and sincere friendship between the United States and their citizens and His Catholic Majesty, his successors and subjects, without exception of persons or places.

ARTICLE II

His Catholic Majesty cedes to the United States, in full property and sovereignty, all the territories which belong to him, situated to the eastward of the Mississippi, known by the name of East and West Florida. The adjacent islands dependent on said provinces, all public lots and squares, vacant lands, public edifices, fortifications, barracks, and other buildings, which are not private property, archives and documents, which relate directly to the property and sovereignty of said provinces, are included in this article. The said archives and documents shall be left in possession of the commissaries or officers of the United States, duly authorized to receive them.

ARTICLE III

The boundary-line between the two countries, west of the Mississippi, shall begin on the Gulph of Mexico, at the mouth of the river Sabine, in the sea, continuing north, along the western bank of that river, to the 32d degree of latitude; thence, by a line due north, to the degree of latitude where it strikes the Rio Roxo of Nachitoches, or Red River; then following the course of the Rio Roxo westward, to the degree of longitude 100 west from London and 23 from Washington; then, crossing the said Red River, and running thence, by a line due north, to the river Arkansas; thence, following the course of the southern bank of the Arkansas, to its source, in latitude 42 north; and thence, by that parallel of latitude, to the South Sea. The whole being as laid down in Melish's map of the United States, published at Philadelphia, improved to the first of January, 1818. But if the source of the Arkansas River shall be found to fall north or south of latitude 42, then the line shall run from the said source due south or north, as the case may be, till it meets the said parallel of latitude 42, and thence, along the said parallel, to the South Sea: All the islands in the Sabine, and the said Red and Arkansas Rivers, throughout the course thus described, to belong to the United States; but the use of the waters, and the navigation of the Sabine to the sea, and of the said rivers Roxo and Arkansas, throughout the extent of the said boundary, on their respective banks, shall be common to the respective inhabitants of both nations.

The two high contracting parties agree to cede and renounce all their rights, claims, and pretensions to the territories described by the said line, that is to say: The United States hereby cede to His Catholic Majesty, and renounce forever, all their rights, claims, and pretensions, to the territories lying west and south of the above-described line; and, in like manner, His Catholic Majesty cedes to the said United States all his rights, claims, and pretensions to any territories east and north of the said line, and for himself, his heirs, and successors, renounces all claim to the said territories forever.

ARTICLE IV

To fix this line with more precision, and to place the landmarks which shall designate exactly the limits of both nations, each of the contracting parties shall appoint a Commissioner and a surveyor, who shall meet before the termination of one year from the date of the ratification of this treaty at Nachitoches, on the Red River, and proceed to run and mark the said line, from the mouth of the Sabine to the Red River, and from the Red River to the river Arkansas, and to ascertain the latitude of the source of the said river Arkansas, in conformity to what is above agreed upon and stipulated and the line of latitude 42, to the South Sea: they shall make out plans, and keep journals of their proceedings, and the result agreed upon by them shall be considered as part of this treaty, and shall have the same force as if it were inserted therein. The two Governments will amicably agree respecting the necessary articles to be furnished to those persons, and also as to their respective escorts, should such be deemed necessary.

ARTICLE V

The inhabitants of the ceded territories shall be secured in the free exercise of their religion, without any restriction; and all those who may desire to remove to the Spanish dominions shall be permitted to sell or export their effects, at any time whatever, without being subject, in either case, to duties.

ARTICLE VI

The inhabitants of the territories which His Catholic Majesty cedes to the United States, by this treaty, shall be incorporated in the Union of the United States as soon as may be consistent with the principles of the Federal Constitution, and admitted to the enjoyment of all the privileges, rights, and immunities of the citizens of the United States.

ARTICLE VII

The officers and troops of His Catholic Majesty, in the territories hereby ceded by him to the United States, shall be withdrawn, and possession of the places occupied by them shall be given within six months after the exchange of the ratifications of this treaty, or sooner if possible, by the officers of His Catholic Majesty to the commissioners or officers of the United States duly appointed to receive them; and the United States shall furnish the transports and escort necessary to convey the Spanish officers and troops and their baggage to the Havana.

ARTICLE VIII

All the grants of land made before the 24th of January, 1818, by His Catholic Majesty, or by his lawful authorities, in the said territories ceded by His Majesty to the United States, shall be ratified and confirmed to the persons in possession of the lands, to the same extent that the same grants would be valid if the territories had remained under the dominion of His Catholic Majesty. But the owners in possession of such lands, who, by reason of the recent circumstances of the Spanish nation, and the revolutions in Europe, have been prevented from fulfilling all the conditions of their grants, shall complete them within the terms limited in the same, respectively, from the date of this treaty; in default of which the said grants shall be null and void. All grants made since the said 24th of January, 1818, when the first proposal, on the part of His Catholic Majesty, for the cession of the Floridas was made, are hereby declared and agreed to be null and void.

ARTICLE IX

The two high contracting parties, animated with the most earnest desire of conciliation, and with the object of putting an end to all the differences which have existed between them, and of confirming the good understanding which they wish to be forever maintained between them, reciprocally renounce all claims for damages or injuries which they, themselves, as well as their respective citizens and subjects, may have suffered until the time of signing this treaty.

1. The renunciation of the United States will extend to all the injuries mentioned in the convention of the 11th of August, 1802.
2. To all claims on account of prizes made by French privateers, and condemned by French Consuls, within the territory and jurisdiction of Spain.
3. To all claims of indemnities on account of the suspension of the right of deposit at New Orleans in 1802.
4. To all claims of citizens of the United States upon the Government of Spain, arising from the unlawful seizures at sea, and in the ports and territories of Spain, or the Spanish colonies.
5. To all claims of citizens of the United States upon the Spanish Government, statements of which, soliciting the interposition of the Government of the United States have been presented to the Department of State, or to the Minister of the United States in Spain, the date of the convention of 1802 and until the signature of this treaty.

The renunciation of His Catholic Majesty extends ––

1. To all the injuries mentioned in the convention of the 11th of August, 1802.
2. To the sums which His Catholic Majesty advanced for the return of Captain Pike from the Provincias Internas.
3. To all injuries caused by the expedition of Miranda, that was fitted out and equipped at New York.
4. To all claims of Spanish subjects upon the Government of the United States arizing from unlawful seizures at sea, or within the ports and territorial Jurisdiction of the United States.

Finally, to all the claims of subjects of His Catholic Majesty upon the Government of the United States in which the interposition of his Catholic Majesty's Government has been solicited, before the date of this treaty and since the date of the convention of 1802, or which may have been made to the department of foreign affairs of His Majesty, or to his Minister of the United States.

And the high contracting parties, respectively, renounce all claim to indemnities for any of the recent events or transactions of their respective commanders and officers in the Floridas.

The United States will cause satisfaction to be made for the injuries, if any, which, by process of law, shall be established to have been suffered by the Spanish officers, and individual Spanish inhabitants, by the late operations of the American Army in Florida.

ARTICLE X

The convention entered into between the two Governments, on the 11th of August, 1802, the ratifications of which were exchanged the 21st December, 1818, is annulled.

ARTICLE XI

The United States, exonerating Spain from all demands in future, on account of the claims of their citizens to which the renunciations herein contained extend, and considering them entirely cancelled, undertake to make satisfaction for the same, to an amount not exceeding five millions of dollars. To ascertain the full amount and validity of those claims, a commission, to consist of three Commissioners, citizens of the United States, shall be appointed by the President, by and with the advice and consent of the Senate, which commission shall meet at the city of Washington, and, within the space of three years from the time of their first meeting, shall receive, examine, and decide upon the amount and validity of all the claims included within the descriptions above mentioned. The said Commissioners shall take an oath or affirmation, to be entered on the record of their proceedings, for the faithful and diligent discharge of their duties; and, in case of the death, sickness, or necessary absence of any such Commissioner, his place may be supplied by the appointment, as aforesaid, or by the President of the United States, during the recess of the Senate, of another Commissioner in his stead.

The said Commissioners shall be authorized to hear and examine, on oath, every question relative to the said claims, and to receive all suitable authentic testimony concerning the same. And the Spanish Government shall furnish all such documents and elucidations as may be in their possession, for the adjustment of the said claims, according to the principles of justice, the laws of nations, and the stipulations of the treaty between the two parties of 27th October, 1795; the said documents to be specified, when demanded, at the instance of the said Commissioners.

The payment of such claims as may be admitted and adjusted by the said Commissioners, or the major part of them, to an amount not exceeding five millions of dollars, shall be made by the United States, either immediately at their Treasury, or by the creation of stock, bearing an interest of six percent. per annum, payable from the proceeds of sales of public lands within the territories hereby ceded to the United States, or in such other manner as the Congress of the United States may prescribe by law.

The records of the proceedings of the said Commissioners, together with the vouchers and documents produced before them, relative to the claims to be adjusted and decided upon by them, shall, after the close of their transactions, be deposited in the Department of State of the United States; and copies of them, or any part of them, shall be furnished to the Spanish Government, if required' at the demand of the Spanish Minister in the United States.

ARTICLE XII

The treaty of limits and navigation, of 1795, remains confirmed in all and each one of its articles excepting the 2, 3, 4, 21, and the second clause of the 22d article, which, having been altered by this treaty, or having received their entire execution, are no longer valid.

With respect to the 15th article of the same treaty of friendship, limits, and navigation of 1795, in which it is stipulated that the flag shall cover the property, the two high contracting parties agree that this shall be so understood with respect to those powers who recognize this principle; but if either of the two contracting parties shall be at war with a third party, and the other neutral, the flag of the neutral shall cover the property of enemies whose government acknowledge this principle, and not of others.

ARTICLE XIII

Both contracting parties, wishing to favor their mutual commerce, by affording in their ports every necessary assistance to their respective merchant-vessels, have agreed that the sailors who shall desert from their vessels in the ports of the other, shall be arrested and delivered up, at the instance of the consul, who shall prove, nevertheless, that the deserters belonged to the vessels that claimed them, exhibiting the document that is customary in their nation: that is to say, the American Consul in a Spanish port shall exhibit the document known lay the name of articles, and the Spanish Consul in American ports the roll of the vessel; and if the name of the deserter or deserters are claimed shall appear in the one or the other, they shall be arrested, held in custody, and delivered to the vessel to which they shall belong.

ARTICLE XIV

The United States hereby certify that they have not received any compensation from France for the injuries they suffered from her privateers, Consuls, and tribunals on the coasts and in the ports of Spain, for the satisfaction of which provision is made by this treaty; and they will present an authentic statement of the prizes made, and of their true value, that Spain may avail herself of the same in such manner as she may deem just and proper.

ARTICLE XV

The United States, to give to His Catholic Majesty a proof of their desire to cement the relations of amity subsisting between the two nations, and to favor the commerce of the subjects of His Catholic Majesty, agree that Spanish vessels, coming Onisladen only with productions of Spanish growth or manufactures, directly from the ports of Spain, or of her colonies, shall be admitted, for the term of twelve years, to the ports of Pensacola and St. Augustine, in the Floridas, without paying other or higher duties on their cargoes, or of tonnage, than will be paid by the vessels of the United States. During the said term no other nation shall enjoy the same privileges within the ceded territories. The twelve years shall commence three months after the exchange of the ratifications of this treaty.

ARTICLE XVI

The present treaty shall be ratified in due form, by the contracting parties, and the ratifications shall be exchanged in six months from this time, or sooner if possible.

In witness whereof we, the underwritten Plenipotentiaries of the United States of America and of His Catholic Majesty, have signed, by virtue of our powers, the present treaty of amity, settlement, and limits, and have thereunto affixed our seals, respectively.

Done at Washington this twenty-second day of February, one thousand eight hundred and nineteen.

JOHN QUINCY ADAMS. [L. S.]
LUIS DE ONIS. [L. S.]

NOTE

The Transcontinental Treaty was originally known as the Treaty of Adams-Onís until approved by the U.S. Congress in 1821.

LESSON SIX

THE TEXAS ANNEXATION RESOLUTION

Resolution for the Annexation of Texas

(March 1, 1845)

United States Congress

The History[6]

The Texas Annexation of 1845 was the voluntary annexation of the Republic of Texas to the United States of America, becoming the twenty-eighth state. Texas claimed but never controlled parts of present-day Colorado, Kansas, New Mexico, Oklahoma, and Wyoming, which became parts of other territories of the United States in the Compromise of 1850.

Anglo-American immigrants, primarily from the South, began immigrating to Mexican Texas in the early 1820s at the request of the Mexican government, which sought to populate the sparsely inhabited lands of its northern frontier. Anglo-Americans soon became a majority in Texas and eventually became disillusioned with Mexican rule. Coahuila y Texas, a Mexican state of which Texas was a constituent part after 1824, endorsed a plan for gradual emancipation in 1827, which angered many slaveholding settlers who had moved to Texas from the South. For this and other reasons, Texas declared independence from Mexico, resulting in war with Mexico. In 1836, the fighting ended and Sam Houston became the first president of the Republic of Texas, elected on a platform that favored annexation to the United States.

In August 1837, James Freeman, the Texan ambassador to the United States, submitted an annexation proposal to the Van Buren administration. Believing that annexation would lead to war with Mexico, the administration declined Texas' proposal. After the election of Mirabeau B. Lamar, an opponent of annexation, as president of Texas in 1838 and the United States' apprehension regarding annexation, Texas withdrew its offer.

In 1843, President John Tyler came out in support of annexation, entering negotiations with the Republic of Texas for an annexation treaty, which he submitted to the Senate. On 8 June 1844, the treaty was defeated 35 to 16, well below the two-thirds majority necessary for ratification. Of the 29 Whig senators, 28 voted against the treaty with only one Whig, a southerner, supporting it. The Democratic senators were more divided on the issue with six northern Democrats and one southern Democrat opposing the treaty and five northern Democrats and ten southern Democrats supporting it.

James K. Polk, a Democrat and a strong supporter of territorial expansion, was elected president in November 1844 with a mandate to acquire both the Republic of Texas and Oregon

---

[6] Originally published as "Texas Annexation," *Wikipedia*, Wikimedia Foundation, Inc., San Francisco, California, November 2009. For additional information see "Diplomacy and Westward Expansion: The Annexation of Texas (1845)," *Timeline of U.S. Diplomatic History (1830–1860)*, Office of the Historian, Bureau of Public Affairs, U.S. Department of State, Washington, DC, 2004. This agency is listed in the *National Resource Directory* section of this volume.

Country. After the election, the Tyler administration realized that public opinion was in favor of annexation, consulted with President-elect Polk, and set out to accomplish annexation by means of a joint resolution. The resolution declared that Texas would be admitted as a state as long as it approved annexation by 1 January 1846, that it could split itself up into four additional states, and that possession of the Republic's public lands would shift to the state of Texas upon its admission. On 26 February 1845, six days before Polk took office, Congress passed the joint resolution. Not long afterwards, Andrew Jackson Donelson, the American chargé d'affaires in Texas and the nephew of former president Andrew Jackson, presented the American resolution to President Anson Jones of Texas. In July 1845, the Texan Congress endorsed the American annexation offer with only one dissenting vote and began writing a state constitution. The citizens of Texas approved the new constitution and the annexation ordinance in October 1845 and Polk signed the documents formally integrating Texas into the United States on 29 December 1845.

The joint resolution and ordinance of annexation contain language permitting the formation of up to four additional states out of the former territories of the Republic of Texas:

> New States of convenient size not exceeding four in number, in addition to said State of Texas and having sufficient population, may, hereafter by the consent of said State, be formed out of the territory thereof, which shall be entitled to admission under the provisions of the Federal Constitution.

The joint resolution required that if any new states were formed out of Texas' lands, those north of the Missouri Compromise line would become free states and those south of the line could choose whether or not to permit slavery. Article Four of the Constitution prohibits the creation of new states out of existing ones without the consent of both the legislature of that state and of Congress, and the division of Texas into multiple states has never been attempted.

The joint resolution and ordinance of annexation have no language specifying the boundaries of Texas, but only refer in general terms to "the territory properly included within, and rightfully belonging to the Republic of Texas," and state that the new State of Texas, is to be formed "subject to the adjustment by this [U.S.] government of all questions of boundary that may arise with other governments."

According to George Lockhart Rives, "That treaty had been expressly so framed as to leave the boundaries of Texas undefined, and the joint resolution of the following winter was drawn in the same manner. It was hoped that this might open the way to a negotiation, in the course of which the whole subject of the boundaries of Mexico, from the Gulf to the Pacific, might be reconsidered, but these hopes came to nothing."

There was an ongoing border dispute between the Republic of Texas and Mexico prior to annexation. Texas claimed the Rio Grande as its border, while Mexico maintained that it was the Nueces River and did not recognize Texas independence. President James K. Polk ordered General Zachary Taylor to garrison the southern border of Texas, as defined by the former Republic. Taylor moved into Texas, ignoring Mexican demands that he withdraw, and marched as far south as the

Rio Grande, where he began to build a fort near the river's mouth on the Gulf of Mexico. The Mexican government regarded this action as a violation of its sovereignty.

The Republic of Texas never controlled what is now New Mexico. The failed Texas Santa Fe Expedition of 1841 was its only attempt to take that territory. El Paso was only taken under Texas governance by Robert Neighbors in 1850, over four years after annexation; he was not welcomed in New Mexico. Texas continued to claim New Mexico as far as the Rio Grande, supported by the rest of the South, and opposed by the North and by New Mexico itself, until agreeing to today's boundary in the Compromise of 1850.

The original controversy about the legality of the annexation of Texas stems from the fact that Congress approved the annexation of Texas as a territory with a simple majority vote approval instead of annexing the land by Treaty, as was done with Native American lands. After the United States and the Republic of Texas were unable to reach a Treaty agreement, Congress passed a Joint Resolution for Annexing Texas to the United States. The Republic of Texas' Annexation Convention then submitted the Ordinance of Annexation to popular vote in October 1845 and the public approved the measure. This Ordinance of Annexation was submitted and approved by the House and Senate of the United States and signed by the President on December 29, 1845. While this was an awkward, if not unusual, treaty process it was fully accepted by all parties involved, and more importantly all parties performed on those agreements making them legally binding. In addition, the United States Supreme Court decided in the case of *DeLima v. Bidwell*, 182 U.S. 1 (1901), that annexation by joint resolution of Congress is legal.

The Document

Resolution for the Annexation of Texas

Resolved by the Senate and House of Representatives of the United States of America in Congress assembled, That Congress doth consent that the territory properly included within, and rightfully belonging to the Republic of Texas, may be erected into a new state, to be called the state of Texas, with a republican form of government, to be adopted by the people of said republic, by deputies in Convention assembled, with the consent of the existing government, in order that the same may be admitted as one of the states of this Union.

2. And be it further resolved, That the foregoing consent of Congress is given upon the following conditions, and with the following guarantees, to wit: First –– said state to be formed, subject to the adjustment by this government of all questions of boundary that may arise with other governments; and the constitution thereof, with the proper evidence of its adoption by the people of said republic of Texas, shall be transmitted to the President of the United States, to be laid before Congress for its final action, on or before the first day of January, one thousand eight hundred and forty-six. Second –– said state, when admitted into the Union, after ceding to the United States all public edifices, fortifications, barracks, ports and harbors, navy and navy-yards, docks, magazines, arms, armaments, and all other property and means pertaining to the public

defence belonging to said republic of Texas, shall retain all the public funds, debts, taxes, and dues of every kind which may belong to or be due and owing said republic; and shall also retain all the vacant and unappropriated lands lying within its limits, to be applied to the payment of the debts and liabilities of said republic of Texas; and the residue of said lands, after discharging said debts and liabilities, to be disposed of as said state may direct; but in no event are said debts and liabilities to become a charge upon the government of the United States. Third — New states, of convenient size, not exceeding four in number, in addition to said state of Texas, and having sufficient population, may hereafter, by the consent of said state, be formed out of the territory thereof, which shall be entitled to admission under the provisions of the federal constitution. And such states as may be formed out of that portion of said territory lying south of thirty-six degrees thirty minutes north latitude, commonly known as the Missouri Compromise line, shall be admitted into the Union with or without slavery, as the people of each state asking admission may desire. And in such state or states as shall be formed out of said territory north of said Missouri compromise line, slavery, or involuntary servitude, (except for crime,) shall be prohibited.

3. And be it further resolved, That if the President of the United States shall in his judgment and discretion deem it most advisable, instead of proceeding to submit the foregoing resolution to the Republic of Texas, as an overture on the part of the United States for admission, to negotiate with that Republic; then,

Be it resolved, that a state, to be formed out of the present Republic of Texas, with suitable extent and boundaries, and with two representatives in Congress, until the next apportionment of representation, shall be admitted into the Union, by virtue of this act, on an equal footing with the existing states, as soon as the terms and conditions of such admission, and the cession of the remaining Texan territory to the United States shall be agreed upon by the governments of Texas and the United States: And that the sum of one hundred thousand dollars be, and the same is hereby, appropriated to defray the expenses of missions and negotiations, to agree upon the terms of said admission and cession, either by treaty to be submitted to the Senate, or by articles to be submitted to the two Houses of Congress, as the President may direct.

Approved, March 1, 1845

Ordinance for the Annexation of Texas

AN ORDINANCE

Whereas,

the Congress of the United States of America has passed resolutions providing for the annexation of Texas to that Union, which resolutions were offered by the President of the United States on the first day of March, 1845; and

Whereas,

> the President of the United States has submitted to Texas the first and second
> sections of said resolutions, as the basis upon which Texas may be admitted as
> one of the States of the said Union; and

Whereas,

> the existing Government of the Republic of Texas, has assented to the proposals
> thus made, –– the terms and conditions of which are as follows:

Joint Resolutions for annexing Texas to the United States

Resolved by the Senate and House of Representatives of the United States of America in Congress assembled, That Congress doth consent that the territory properly included within, and rightfully belonging to the Republic of Texas, may be erected into a new state, to be called the state of Texas, with a republican form of government, to be adopted by the people of said republic, by deputies in Convention assembled, with the consent of the existing government, in order that the same may be admitted as one of the States of this Union.

2nd. And be it further resolved, That the foregoing consent of Congress is given upon the following conditions, and with the following guarantees, to wit: First, said state to be formed, subject to the adjustment by this government of all questions of boundary that may arise with other governments; and the constitution thereof, with the proper evidence of its adoption by the people of said republic of Texas, shall be transmitted to the President of the United States, to be laid before Congress for its final action, on or before the first day of January, one thousand eight hundred and forty-six. Second, said state, when admitted into the Union, after ceding to the United States all public edifices, fortifications, barracks, ports and harbors, navy and navy-yards, docks, magazines, arms, armaments, and all other property and means pertaining to the public defence belonging to said republic of Texas, shall retain all the public funds, debts, taxes, and dues of every kind which may belong to or be due and owing said republic; and shall also retain all the vacant and unappropriated lands lying within its limits, to be applied to the payment of the debts and liabilities of said republic of Texas; and the residue of said lands, after discharging said debts and liabilities, to be disposed of as said state may direct; but in no event are said debts and liabilities to become a charge upon the government of the United States. Third –– New states, of convenient size, not exceeding four in number, in addition to said state of Texas, and having sufficient population, may hereafter, by the consent of said state, be formed out of the territory thereof, which shall be entitled to admission under the provisions of the federal constitution. And such states as may be formed out of that portion of said territory lying south of thirty-six degrees thirty minutes north latitude, commonly known as the Missouri compromise line, shall be admitted into the Union with or without slavery, as the people of each state asking admission may desire. And in such state or states as shall be formed out of said territory north of said Missouri compromise line, slavery, or involuntary servitude, (except for crime,) shall be prohibited.

Now in order to manifest the assent of the people of this Republic, as required in the above recited portions of said resolutions, we the deputies of the people of Texas, in convention assembled, in their name and in their authority, do ordain and declare, that we assent to and accept the proposals, conditions and guarantees, contained in the first and second sections of the Resolution of the Congress of the United States aforesaid.

In testimony whereof, we have hereunto subscribed our names

Thomas J. Rusk
President

followed by 61 signatures

Attest
James H. Raymond
Secretary of the Convention

Approved on July 4, 1845

LESSON SEVEN

THE OREGON TERRITORY TREATY

Oregon Treaty

(June 15, 1846)

United States Congress

The History[7]

The Oregon Treaty is a treaty between the United Kingdom of Great Britain and Ireland and the United States that was signed on June 15, 1846, in Washington, D.C. The treaty brought an end to the Oregon boundary dispute by settling competing American and British claims to the Oregon Country, which had been jointly occupied by both Britain and the U.S. since the Treaty of 1818.

The Treaty of 1818 set the boundary between the United States and British North America along the 49th parallel of north latitude from Minnesota to the "Stony Mountains" (now know as the Rocky Mountains). West of those mountains was known to the Americans as the Oregon Country and to the British as the Columbia Department or Columbia District of the Hudson's Bay Company. (Also included in the region was the southern portion of another fur district, New Caledonia.) The treaty provided for joint control of that land for ten years. Both countries could claim land and both were guaranteed free navigation throughout.

Joint control steadily grew less tolerable for both sides. After a British minister rejected U.S. President James K. Polk's offer to settle the boundary at the 49th parallel north, Democratic expansionists called for the annexation of the entire region up to 54°40', the southern limit of Russian America as established by parallel treaties between the Russian Empire and the U.S. (1824) and Britain (1825). However, after the outbreak of the Mexican-American War diverted U.S. attention and resources, a compromise was reached.

The treaty was negotiated by U.S. Secretary of State James Buchanan, who later became president; and Richard Pakenham, British envoy to the United States and member of the Privy Council of the United Kingdom for Queen Victoria. The treaty was signed on June 15, 1846.

The Oregon Treaty set the U.S. and British North American border at the 49th parallel with the exception of Vancouver Island, which was retained in its entirety by the British. Vancouver Island, with all coastal islands, was constituted as the Colony of Vancouver Island in 1849. The U.S. portion of the region was organized as Oregon Territory on August 14, 1848, with Washington Territory being formed from it in 1853. The British portion remained unorganized until 1858 when the Colony of British Columbia was declared as a result of the Fraser Canyon

---

[7] Originally published as "Oregon Treaty," *Wikipedia*, Wikimedia Foundation, Inc., San Francisco, California, November 2009. For additional information see "Diplomacy and Westward Expansion: The Oregon Territory (1846)," *Timeline of U.S. Diplomatic History (1830–1860)*, Office of the Historian, Bureau of Public Affairs, U.S. Department of State, Washington, DC, 2004. This agency is listed in the *National Resource Directory* section of this volume.

Gold Rush and fears of reasserted American expansionist intentions. The two British colonies were amalgamated in 1866 as the Colony of British Columbia. When the Colony of British Columbia joined Canada in 1871, the 49th Parallel and marine boundaries established by the Oregon Treaty became the U.S.–Canadian border.

The treaty defined the border in the Strait of June de Fuca through the major channel. Unfortunately, the "major channel" was not defined.

- Navigation of "channel[s] and straits, south of the forty-ninth parallel of north latitude, remain free and open to both parties."
- The "Puget's Sound Agricultural Company" retains the right to their property north of the Columbia River, and shall be compensated for properties surrendered if required by the United States. (The Puget's Sound Agricultural Company was a subsidiary of the Hudson's Bay Company).
- The property rights of the Hudson's Bay Company and all British subjects south of the new boundary will be respected.

In 1859, an unclear description of the maritime border in the treaty led to the bloodless war known as the Pig War over the ownership of the San Juan Islands.

The Document

Oregon Treaty[1]

THE United States of America and her Majesty the Queen of the United Kingdom of Great Britain and Ireland, deeming it to be desirable for the future welfare of both countries that the state of doubt and uncertainty which has hitherto prevailed respecting the sovereignty and government of the territory on the northwest coast of America, lying westward of the Rocky or Stony Mountains, should be finally terminated by an amicable compromise of the rights mutually asserted by the two parties over the said territory, have respectively named plenipotentiaries to treat and agree concerning the terms of such settlement – that is to say: the President of the United States of America has, on his part, furnished with full powers James Buchanan, Secretary of State of the United States, and her Majesty the Queen of the United Kingdom of Great Britain and Ireland has, on her part, appointed the Right Honorable Richard Pakenham, a member of her Majesty's Most Honorable Privy Council, and her Majesty's Envoy Extraordinary and Minister Plenipotentiary to the United States; who, after having communicated to each other their respective full powers, found in good and due form, have agreed upon and concluded the following articles: –

ARTICLE I.

From the point on the forty-ninth parallel of north latitude, where the boundary laid down in existing treaties and conventions between the United States and Great Britain terminates, the line of boundary between the territories of the United States and those of her Britannic Majesty shall be continued westward along the said forty-ninth parallel of north latitude to the middle of the channel which separates the continent from Vancouver's Island, and thence southerly through the middle of the said channel, and of Fuca's Straits, to the Pacific Ocean: Provided, however, That the navigation of the whole of the said channel and straits, south of the forty-ninth parallel of north latitude, remain free and open to both parties.

ARTICLE II.

From the point at which the forty-ninth parallel of north latitude shall be found to intersect the great northern branch of the Columbia River, the navigation of the said branch shall be free and open to the Hudson's Bay Company, and to all British subjects trading with the same, to the point where the said branch meets the main stream of the Columbia, and thence down the said main stream to the ocean, with Fee access into and through the said river or rivers, it being understood that all the usual portages along the line thus described shall, in like manner, be free and open. In navigating the said river or rivers, British subjects, with their goods and produce, shall be treated on the same footing as citizens of the United States; it being, however, always understood that nothing in this article shall be construed as preventing, or intended to prevent, the government of the United States from making any regulations respecting the navigation of the said river or rivers not inconsistent with the present treaty.

ARTICLE III.

In the future appropriation of the territory south of the forty-ninth parallel of north latitude, as provided in the first article of this treaty, the possessory rights of the Hudson's Bay Company, and of all British subjects who may be already in the occupation of land or other property lawfully acquired within the said territory, shall be respected.

ARTICLE IV.

The farms, lands, and other property of every description, belonging to the Puget's Sound Agricultural Company, on the north side of the Columbia River, shall be confirmed to the said company. In case, however, the situation of those farms and lands should be considered by the United States to be of public and political importance, and the United States government should signify a desire to obtain possession of the whole, or of any part thereof, the property so required shall be transferred to the said government, at a proper valuation, to be agreed upon between the parties.

ARTICLE V.

The present treaty shall be ratified by the President of the United States, by and with the advice and consent of the Senate thereof, and by her Britannic Majesty; and the ratifications shall be exchanged at London, at the expiration of six months from the date hereof, or sooner, if possible.

In witness whereof, the respective Plenipotentiaries have signed the same, and have affixed thereto the seals of their arms.

Done at Washington, the fifteenth day of June, in the year of our Lord one thousand eight hundred and forty-six.

JAMES BUCHANAN [L S.]
RICHARD PAKENHAM [L. S.]

NOTE

1. Officially titled the *Treaty between Her Majesty and the United States of America, for the Settlement of the Oregon Boundary* and styled in the United States as the *Treaty with Great Britain, in Regard to Limits Westward of the Rocky Mountains*, and also known as the *Buchanan-Pakenham* (or *Packenham*) *Treaty* or (sharing the name with several other unrelated treaties) the *Treaty of Washington*.

LESSON EIGHT

THE SOUTHERN MEXICO TERRITORY TREATY

Treaty of Guadalupe Hidalgo

(February 2, 1848)

United States Congress

▌The History[8]

The Treaty of Guadalupe Hidalgo which brought an official end to the Mexican-American War (1846–1848) was signed on February 2, 1848, at Guadalupe Hidalgo, a city north of the capital where the Mexican government had fled with the advance of U.S. forces.

With the defeat of its army and the fall of the capital, Mexico City, in September 1847 the Mexican government surrendered to the United States and entered into negotiations to end the way. The peace talks were negotiated by Nicholas Trist, chief clerk of the State Department, who had accompanied General Winfield Scott as a diplomat and President Polk's representative. Trist and General Scott, after two previous unsuccessful attempts to negotiate a treaty with Santa Anna, determined that the only way to deal with Mexico was as a conquered enemy. Nicholas Trist negotiated with a special commission representing the collapsed government led by Don Bernardo Couto, Don Miguel Atristain, and Don Luis Gonzaga Cuevas of Mexico.

Under the terms of the treaty negotiated by Trist, Mexico ceded to the United States Upper California and New Mexico. This was known as the Mexican Cession and included present-day Arizona and New Mexico and parts of Utah, Nevada, and Colorado (see Article V of the treaty). Mexico relinquished all claims to Texas and recognized the Rio Grande as the southern boundary with the United States (see Article V).

The United States paid Mexico $15,000,000 "in consideration of the extension acquired by the boundaries of the United States" (see Article XII of the treaty) and agreed to pay American citizens' debts owed to them by the Mexican government (see Article XV). Other provisions included protection of property and civil rights of Mexican nationals living within the new boundaries of the United States (see Articles VIII and IX), the promise of the United States to police its boundaries (see Article XI), and compulsory arbitration of future disputes between the two countries (see Article XXI).

Trist sent a copy to Washington by the fastest means available, forcing Polk to decide whether or not to repudiate the highly satisfactory handiwork of his discredited subordinate. Polk chose to forward the treaty to the Senate. When the Senate reluctantly ratified the treaty (by a vote of

---

[8] Originally published as "Teaching with Documents: The Treaty of Guadalupe Hidalgo," *Educators and Students Report*, The National Archives, U.S. National Archives and Records Administration, College Park, Maryland, 2009. For additional information see "Diplomacy and Westward Expansion: The Treaty of Guadalupe Hidalgo (1848), *Timeline of U.S. Diplomatic History (1830–1860)*, Office of the Historian, Bureau of Public Affairs, U.S. Department of State, Washington, DC, 2004. This agency is listed in the *National Resource Directory* section of this volume.

34 to 14) on March 10, 1848, it deleted Article X guaranteeing the protection of Mexican land grants. Following the ratification, U.S. troops were removed from the Mexican capital.

To carry the treaty into effect, commissioner Colonel Jon Weller and surveyor Andrew Grey were appointed by the United States government and General Pedro Conde and Sr. Jose Illarregui were appointed by the Mexican government to survey and set the boundary. A subsequent treaty of December 30, 1853, altered the border from the initial one by adding 47 more boundary markers to the original six. Of the 53 markers, the majority were rude piles of stone; a few were of durable character with proper inscriptions.

Over time, markers were moved or destroyed, resulting in two subsequent conventions (1882 and 1889) between the two countries to more clearly define the boundaries. Photographers were brought in to document the location of the markers. These photographs are in Record Group 77, Records of the Office of the Chief Engineers, in the National Archives.

The Document

Treaty of Guadalupe Hidalgo

In the Name of Almighty God

The United States of America and the United Mexican States animated by a sincere desire to put an end to the calamities of the war which unhappily exists between the two Republics and to establish Upon a solid basis relations of peace and friendship, which shall confer reciprocal benefits upon the citizens of both, and assure the concord, harmony, and mutual confidence wherein the two people should live, as good neighbors have for that purpose appointed their respective plenipotentiaries, that is to say: The President of the United States has appointed Nicholas P. Trist, a citizen of the United States, and the President of the Mexican Republic has appointed Don Luis Gonzaga Cuevas, Don Bernardo Couto, and Don Miguel Atristain, citizens of the said Republic; Who, after a reciprocal communication of their respective full powers, have, under the protection of Almighty God, the author of peace, arranged, agreed upon, and signed the following: Treaty of Peace, Friendship, Limits, and Settlement between the United States of America and the Mexican Republic.

ARTICLE I

There shall be firm and universal peace between the United States of America and the Mexican Republic, and between their respective countries, territories, cities, towns, and people, without exception of places or persons.

ARTICLE II

Immediately upon the signature of this treaty, a convention shall be entered into between a commissioner or commissioners appointed by the General-in-chief of the forces of the United States, and such as may be appointed by the Mexican Government, to the end that a provisional suspension of hostilities shall take place, and that, in the places occupied by the said forces, constitutional order may be reestablished, as regards the political, administrative, and judicial branches, so far as this shall be permitted by the circumstances of military occupation.

ARTICLE III

Immediately upon the ratification of the present treaty by the Government of the United States, orders shall be transmitted to the commanders of their land and naval forces, requiring the latter (provided this treaty shall then have been ratified by the Government of the Mexican Republic, and the ratifications exchanged) immediately to desist from blockading any Mexican ports and requiring the former (under the same condition) to commence, at the earliest moment practicable, withdrawing all troops of the United States then in the interior of the Mexican Republic, to points that shall be selected by common agreement, at a distance from the seaports not exceeding thirty leagues; and such evacuation of the interior of the Republic shall be completed with the least possible delay; the Mexican Government hereby binding itself to afford every facility in its power for rendering the same convenient to the troops, on their march and in their new positions, and for promoting a good understanding between them and the inhabitants. In like manner orders shall be despatched to the persons in charge of the custom houses at all ports occupied by the forces of the United States, requiring them (under the same condition) immediately to deliver possession of the same to the persons authorized by the Mexican Government to receive it, together with all bonds and evidences of debt for duties on importations and on exportations, not yet fallen due. Moreover, a faithful and exact account shall be made out, showing the entire amount of all duties on imports and on exports, collected at such custom-houses, or elsewhere in Mexico, by authority of the United States, from and after the day of ratification of this treaty by the Government of the Mexican Republic; and also an account of the cost of collection; and such entire amount, deducting only the cost of collection, shall be delivered to the Mexican Government, at the city of Mexico, within three months after the exchange of ratifications.

The evacuation of the capital of the Mexican Republic by the troops of the United States, in virtue of the above stipulation, shall be completed in one month after the orders there stipulated for shall have been received by the commander of said troops, or sooner if possible.

ARTICLE IV

Immediately after the exchange of ratifications of the present treaty all castles, forts, territories, places, and possessions, which have been taken or occupied by the forces of the United States during the present war, within the limits of the Mexican Republic, as about to be established by the following article, shall be definitely restored to the said Republic, together with all the artillery, arms, apparatus of war, munitions, and other public property, which were in the said castles and forts when captured, and which shall remain there at the time when this treaty shall be duly ratified by the Government of the Mexican Republic. To this end, immediately upon the signature of this treaty, orders shall be despatched to the American officers commanding such castles and forts, securing against the removal or destruction of any such artillery, arms, apparatus of war, munitions, or other public property. The city of Mexico, within the inner line of intrenchments surrounding the said city, is comprehended in the above stipulation, as regards the restoration of artillery, apparatus of war, & c.

The final evacuation of the territory of the Mexican Republic, by the forces of the United States, shall be completed in three months from the said exchange of ratifications, or sooner if possible; the Mexican Government hereby engaging, as in the foregoing article, to use all means in its power for facilitating such evacuation, and rendering it convenient to the troops, and for promoting a good understanding between them and the inhabitants.

If, however, the ratification of this treaty by both parties should not take place in time to allow the embarcation of the troops of the United States to be completed before the commencement of the sickly season, at the Mexican ports on the Gulf of Mexico, in such case a friendly arrangement shall be entered into between the General-in-Chief of the said troops and the Mexican Government, whereby healthy and otherwise suitable places, at a distance from the ports not exceeding thirty leagues, shall be designated for the residence of such troops as may not yet have embarked, until the return of the healthy season. And the space of time here referred to as, comprehending the sickly season shall be understood to extend from the first day of May to the first day of November.

All prisoners of war taken on either side, on land or on sea, shall be restored as soon as practicable after the exchange of ratifications of this treaty. It is also agreed that if any Mexicans should now be held as captives by any savage tribe within the limits of the United States, as about to be established by the following article, the Government of the said United States will exact the release of such captives and cause them to be restored to their country.

ARTICLE V

The boundary line between the two Republics shall commence in the Gulf of Mexico, three leagues from land, opposite the mouth of the Rio Grande, otherwise called Rio Bravo del Norte, or Opposite the mouth of its deepest branch, if it should have more than one branch emptying directly into the sea; from thence up the middle of that river, following the deepest channel, where it has more than one, to the point where it strikes the southern boundary of New Mexico; thence, westwardly, along the whole southern boundary of New Mexico (which runs north of the town called Paso) to its western termination; thence, northward, along the western line of New Mexico, until it intersects the first branch of the river Gila; (or if it should not intersect any branch of that river, then to the point on the said line nearest to such branch, and thence in a direct line to the same); thence down the middle of the said branch and of the said river, until it empties into the Rio Colorado; thence across the Rio Colorado, following the division line between Upper and Lower California, to the Pacific Ocean.

The southern and western limits of New Mexico, mentioned in the article, are those laid down in the map entitled "Map of the United Mexican States, as organized and defined by various acts of the Congress of said republic, and constructed according to the best authorities. Revised edition. Published at New York, in 1847, by J. Disturnell," of which map a copy is added to this treaty, bearing the signatures and seals of the undersigned Plenipotentiaries. And, in order to preclude all difficulty in tracing upon the ground the limit separating Upper from Lower California, it is agreed that the said limit shall consist of a straight line drawn from the middle of the Rio Gila, where it unites with the Colorado, to a point on the coast of the Pacific Ocean, distant one marine league due south of the southernmost point of the port of San Diego, according to the plan of said port made in the year 1782 by Don Juan Pantoja, second sailing-master of the Spanish fleet, and published at Madrid in the year 1802, in the atlas to the voyage of the schooners Sutil and Mexicana; of which plan a copy is hereunto added, signed and sealed by the respective Plenipotentiaries.

In order to designate the boundary line with due precision, upon authoritative maps, and to establish upon the ground land-marks which shall show the limits of both republics, as described in the present article, the two Governments shall each appoint a commissioner and a surveyor, who, before the expiration of one year from the date of the exchange of ratifications of this treaty, shall meet at the port of San Diego, and proceed to run and mark the said boundary in its whole course to the mouth of the Rio Bravo del Norte. They shall keep journals and make out plans of their operations; and the result agreed upon by them shall be deemed a part of this treaty, and shall have the same force as if it were inserted therein. The two Governments will amicably agree regarding what may be necessary to these persons, and also as to their respective escorts, should such be necessary.

The boundary line established by this article shall be religiously respected by each of the two republics, and no change shall ever be made therein, except by the express and free consent of both nations, lawfully given by the General Government of each, in conformity with its own constitution.

ARTICLE VI

The vessels and citizens of the United States shall, in all time, have a free and uninterrupted passage by the Gulf of California, and by the river Colorado below its confluence with the Gila, to and from their possessions situated north of the boundary line defined in the preceding article; it being understood that this passage is to be by navigating the Gulf of California and the river Colorado, and not by land, without the express consent of the Mexican Government.

If, by the examinations which may be made, it should be ascertained to be practicable and advantageous to construct a road, canal, or railway, which should in whole or in part run upon the river Gila, or upon its right or its left bank, within the space of one marine league from either margin of the river, the Governments of both republics will form an agreement regarding its construction, in order that it may serve equally for the use and advantage of both countries.

ARTICLE VII

The river Gila, and the part of the Rio Bravo del Norte lying below the southern boundary of New Mexico, being, agreeably to the fifth article, divided in the middle between the two republics, the navigation of the Gila and of the Bravo below said boundary shall be free and common to the vessels and citizens of both countries; and neither shall, without the consent of the other, construct any work that may impede or interrupt, in whole or in part, the exercise of this right; not even for the purpose of favoring new methods of navigation. Nor shall any tax or contribution, under any denomination or title, be levied upon vessels or persons navigating the same or upon merchandise or effects transported thereon, except in the case of landing upon one of their shores. If, for the purpose of making the said rivers navigable, or for maintaining them in such state, it should be necessary or advantageous to establish any tax or contribution, this shall not be done without the consent of both Governments.

The stipulations contained in the present article shall not impair the territorial rights of either republic within its established limits.

ARTICLE VIII

Mexicans now established in territories previously belonging to Mexico, and which remain for the future within the limits of the United States, as defined by the present treaty, shall be free to continue where they now reside, or to remove at any time to the Mexican Republic, retaining the property which they possess in the said territories, or disposing thereof, and removing the proceeds wherever they please, without their being subjected, on this account, to any contribution, tax, or charge whatever.

Those who shall prefer to remain in the said territories may either retain the title and rights of Mexican citizens, or acquire those of citizens of the United States. But they shall be under the obligation to make their election within one year from the date of the exchange of ratifications of this treaty; and those who shall remain in the said territories after the expiration of that year, without having declared their intention to retain the character of Mexicans, shall be considered to have elected to become citizens of the United States.

In the said territories, property of every kind, now belonging to Mexicans not established there, shall be inviolably respected. The present owners, the heirs of these, and all Mexicans who may hereafter acquire said property by contract, shall enjoy with respect to it guarantees equally ample as if the same belonged to citizens of the United States.

ARTICLE IX

The Mexicans who, in the territories aforesaid, shall not preserve the character of citizens of the Mexican Republic, conformably with what is stipulated in the preceding article, shall be incorporated into the Union of the United States and be admitted at the proper time (to be judged of by the Congress of the United States) to the enjoyment of all the rights of citizens of the United States, according to the principles of the Constitution; and in the mean time, shall be maintained and protected in the free enjoyment of their liberty and property, and secured in the free exercise of their religion without restriction.

ARTICLE X

[Stricken out]

ARTICLE XI

Considering that a great part of the territories, which, by the present treaty, are to be comprehended for the future within the limits of the United States, is now occupied by savage tribes, who will hereafter be under the exclusive control of the Government of the United States, and whose incursions within the territory of Mexico would be prejudicial in the extreme, it is solemnly agreed that all such incursions shall be forcibly restrained by the Government of the United States whensoever this may be necessary; and that when they cannot be prevented, they shall be punished by the said Government, and satisfaction for the same shall be exacted all in the same way, and with equal diligence and energy, as if the same incursions were meditated or committed within its own territory, against its own citizens.

It shall not be lawful, under any pretext whatever, for any inhabitant of the United States to purchase or acquire any Mexican, or any foreigner residing in Mexico, who may have been captured by Indians inhabiting the territory of either of the two republics; nor to purchase or acquire horses, mules, cattle, or property of any kind, stolen within Mexican territory by such Indians.

And in the event of any person or persons, captured within Mexican territory by Indians, being carried into the territory of the United States, the Government of the latter engages and binds itself, in the most solemn manner, so soon as it shall know of such captives being within its territory, and shall be able so to do, through the faithful exercise of its influence and power, to rescue them and return them to their country, or deliver them to the agent or representative of the Mexican Government. The Mexican authorities will, as far as practicable, give to the Government of the United States notice of such captures; and its agents shall pay the expenses incurred in the maintenance and transmission of the rescued captives; who, in the mean time, shall be treated with the utmost hospitality by the American authorities at the place where they may be. But if the Government of the United States, before receiving such notice from Mexico, should obtain intelligence, through any other channel, of the existence of Mexican captives within its territory, it will proceed forthwith to effect their release and delivery to the Mexican agent, as above stipulated.

For the purpose of giving to these stipulations the fullest possible efficacy, thereby affording the security and redress demanded by their true spirit and intent, the Government of the United States will now and hereafter pass, without unnecessary delay, and always vigilantly enforce, such laws as the nature of the subject may require. And, finally, the sacredness of this obligation shall never be lost sight of by the said Government, when providing for the removal of the Indians from any portion of the said territories, or for its being settled by citizens of the United States;

but, on the contrary, special care shall then be taken not to place its Indian occupants under the necessity of seeking new homes, by committing those invasions which the United States have solemnly obliged themselves to restrain.

ARTICLE XII

In consideration of the extension acquired by the boundaries of the United States, as defined in the fifth article of the present treaty, the Government of the United States engages to pay to that of the Mexican Republic the sum of fifteen millions of dollars.

Immediately after the treaty shall have been duly ratified by the Government of the Mexican Republic, the sum of three millions of dollars shall be paid to the said Government by that of the United States, at the city of Mexico, in the gold or silver coin of Mexico. The remaining twelve millions of dollars shall be paid at the same place, and in the same coin, in annual installments of three millions of dollars each, together with interest on the same at the rate of six per centum per annum. This interest shall begin to run upon the whole sum of twelve millions from the day of the ratification of the present treaty by – the Mexican Government, and the first of the installments shall be paid – at the expiration of one year from the same day. Together with each annual installment, as it falls due, the whole interest accruing on such installment from the beginning shall also be paid.

ARTICLE XIII

The United States engage, moreover, to assume and pay to the claimants all the amounts now due them, and those hereafter to become due, by reason of the claims already liquidated and decided against the Mexican Republic, under the conventions between the two republics severally concluded on the eleventh day of April, eighteen hundred and thirty-nine, and on the thirtieth day of January, eighteen hundred and forty-three; so that the Mexican Republic shall be absolutely exempt, for the future, from all expense whatever on account of the said claims.

ARTICLE XIV

The United States do furthermore discharge the Mexican Republic from all claims of citizens of the United States, not heretofore decided against the Mexican Government, which may have arisen previously to the date of the signature of this treaty; which discharge shall be final and perpetual, whether the said claims be rejected or be allowed by the board of commissioners provided for in the following article, and whatever shall be the total amount of those allowed.

ARTICLE XV

The United States, exonerating Mexico from all demands on account of the claims of their citizens mentioned in the preceding article, and considering them entirely and forever canceled, whatever their amount may be, undertake to make satisfaction for the same, to an amount not exceeding three and one-quarter millions of dollars. To ascertain the validity and amount of those claims, a board of commissioners shall be established by the Government of the United States, whose awards shall be final and conclusive; provided that, in deciding upon the validity of each claim, the board shall be guided and governed by the principles and rules of decision prescribed by the first and fifth articles of the unratified convention, concluded at the city of Mexico on the twentieth day of November, one thousand eight hundred and forty-three; and in no case shall an award be made in favour of any claim not embraced by these principles and rules.

If, in the opinion of the said board of commissioners or of the claimants, any books, records, or documents, in the possession or power of the Government of the Mexican Republic, shall be deemed necessary to the just decision of any claim, the commissioners, or the claimants through them, shall, within such period as Congress may designate, make an application in writing for the same, addressed to the Mexican Minister of Foreign Affairs, to be transmitted by the Secretary of State of the United States; and the Mexican Government engages, at the earliest possible moment after the receipt of such demand, to cause any of the books, records, or documents so specified, which shall be in their possession or power (or authenticated copies or extracts of the same), to be transmitted to the said Secretary of State, who shall immediately deliver them over to the said board of commissioners; provided that no such application shall be made by or at the instance of any claimant, until the facts which it is expected to prove by such books, records, or documents, shall have been stated under oath or affirmation.

Article XVI

Each of the contracting parties reserves to itself the entire right to fortify whatever point within its territory it may judge proper so to fortify for its security.

Article XVII

The treaty of amity, commerce, and navigation, concluded at the city of Mexico, on the fifth day of April, A. D. 1831, between the United States of America and the United Mexican States, except the additional article, and except so far as the stipulations of the said treaty may be incompatible with any stipulation contained in the present treaty, is hereby revived for the period of eight years from the day of the exchange of ratifications of this treaty, with the same force and virtue as if incorporated therein; it being understood that each of the contracting parties reserves to itself the right, at any time after the said period of eight years shall have expired, to terminate the same by giving one year's notice of such intention to the other party.

Article XVIII

All supplies whatever for troops of the United States in Mexico, arriving at ports in the occupation of such troops previous to the final evacuation thereof, although subsequently to the restoration of the custom-houses at such ports, shall be entirely exempt from duties and charges of any kind; the Government of the United States hereby engaging and pledging its faith to establish and vigilantly to enforce, all possible guards for securing the revenue of Mexico, by preventing the importation, under cover of this stipulation, of any articles other than such, both in kind and in quantity, as shall really be wanted for the use and consumption of the forces of the United States during the time they may remain in Mexico. To this end it shall be the duty of all officers and agents of the United States to denounce to the Mexican authorities at the respective ports any attempts at a fraudulent abuse of this stipulation, which they may know of, or may have reason to suspect, and to give to such authorities all the aid in their power with regard thereto; and every such attempt, when duly proved and established by sentence of a competent tribunal, They shall be punished by the confiscation of the property so attempted to be fraudulently introduced.

Article XIX

With respect to all merchandise, effects, and property whatsoever, imported into ports of Mexico, whilst in the occupation of the forces of the United States, whether by citizens of either republic, or by citizens or subjects of any neutral nation, the following rules shall be observed:

(1) All such merchandise, effects, and property, if imported previously to the restoration of the custom-houses to the Mexican authorities, as stipulated for in the third article of this treaty, shall be exempt from confiscation, although the importation of the same be prohibited by the Mexican tariff.

(2) The same perfect exemption shall be enjoyed by all such merchandise, effects, and property, imported subsequently to the restoration of the custom-houses, and previously to the sixty days fixed in the following article for the coming into force of the Mexican tariff at such ports respectively; the said merchandise, effects, and property being, however, at the time of their importation, subject to the payment of duties, as provided for in the said following article.

(3) All merchandise, effects, and property described in the two rules foregoing shall, during their continuance at the place of importation, and upon their leaving such place for the interior, be exempt from all duty, tax, or imposts of every kind, under whatsoever title or denomination. Nor shall they be there subject to any charge whatsoever upon the sale thereof.

(4) All merchandise, effects, and property, described in the first and second rules, which shall have been removed to any place in the interior, whilst such place was in the occupation of the forces of the United States, shall, during their continuance therein, be exempt from all tax upon the sale or consumption thereof, and from every kind of impost or contribution, under whatsoever title or denomination.

(5) But if any merchandise, effects, or property, described in the first and second rules, shall be removed to any place not occupied at the time by the forces of the United States, they shall, upon their introduction into such place, or upon their sale or consumption there, be subject to the same duties which, under the Mexican laws, they would be required to pay in such cases if they had been imported in time of peace, through the maritime custom-houses, and had there paid the duties conformably with the Mexican tariff.

(6)   The owners of all merchandise, effects, or property, described in the first and second rules, and existing in any port of Mexico, shall have the right to reship the same, exempt from all tax, impost, or contribution whatever.

With respect to the metals, or other property, exported from any Mexican port whilst in the occupation of the forces of the United States, and previously to the restoration of the custom-house at such port, no person shall be required by the Mexican authorities, whether general or state, to pay any tax, duty, or contribution upon any such exportation, or in any manner to account for the same to the said authorities.

ARTICLE XX

Through consideration for the interests of commerce generally, it is agreed, that if less than sixty days should elapse between the date of the signature of this treaty and the restoration of the custom houses, conformably with the stipulation in the third article, in such case all merchandise, effects and property whatsoever, arriving at the Mexican ports after the restoration of the said custom-houses, and previously to the expiration of sixty days after the day of signature of this treaty, shall be admitted to entry; and no other duties shall be levied thereon than the duties established by the tariff found in force at such custom-houses at the time of the restoration of the same. And to all such merchandise, effects, and property, the rules established by the preceding article shall apply.

Article XXI

If unhappily any disagreement should hereafter arise between the Governments of the two republics, whether with respect to the interpretation of any stipulation in this treaty, or with respect to any other particular concerning the political or commercial relations of the two nations, the said Governments, in the name of those nations, do promise to each other that they will endeavour, in the most sincere and earnest manner, to settle the differences so arising, and to preserve the state of peace and friendship in which the two countries are now placing themselves, using, for this end, mutual representations and pacific negotiations. And if, by these means, they should not be enabled to come to an agreement, a resort shall not, on this account, be had to reprisals, aggression, or hostility of any kind, by the one republic against the other, until the Government of that which deems itself aggrieved shall have maturely considered, in the spirit of peace and good neighbourship, whether it would not be better that such difference should be settled by the arbitration of commissioners appointed on each side, or by that of a friendly nation. And should such course be proposed by either party, it shall be acceded to by the other, unless deemed by it altogether incompatible with the nature of the difference, or the circumstances of the case.

Article XXII

If (which is not to be expected, and which God forbid) war should unhappily break out between the two republics, they do now, with a view to such calamity, solemnly pledge themselves to each other and to the world to observe the following rules; absolutely where the nature of the subject permits, and as closely as possible in all cases where such absolute observance shall be impossible:

(1)   The merchants of either republic then residing in the other shall be allowed to remain twelve months (for those dwelling in the interior), and six months (for those dwelling at the seaports) to collect their debts and settle their affairs; during which periods they shall enjoy the same protection, and be on the same footing, in all respects, as the citizens or subjects of the most friendly nations; and, at the expiration thereof, or at any time before, they shall have full liberty to depart, carrying off all their effects without molestation or hindrance, conforming therein to the same laws which the citizens or subjects of the most friendly nations are required to conform to. Upon the entrance of the armies of either nation into the territories of the other, women and children, ecclesiastics, scholars of every faculty, cultivators of the earth, merchants, artisans, manufacturers, and fishermen, unarmed and inhabiting unfortified towns, villages, or places, and in general all persons whose occupations are for the common subsistence and benefit of mankind, shall be allowed to continue their respective employments, unmolested in their persons. Nor shall their houses or goods be burnt or otherwise destroyed, nor their cattle taken, nor their fields wasted, by the armed force into whose power, by the events of war, they may happen to fall; but if the necessity arise to take anything from them for the use of such armed force, the same shall be paid for at an equitable price. All churches, hospitals, schools, colleges, libraries, and other establishments for charitable and beneficent purposes, shall be respected, and all persons connected with the same protected in the discharge of their duties, and the pursuit of their vocations.

(2)   In order that the fate of prisoners of war may be alleviated all such practices as those of sending them into distant, inclement or unwholesome districts, or crowding them into close and noxious places, shall be studiously avoided. They shall not be confined in dungeons, prison ships, or prisons; nor be put in irons, or bound or otherwise restrained in the use of their limbs. The officers shall enjoy liberty on their paroles, within convenient districts, and have comfortable quarters; and the common soldiers shall be disposed in cantonments, open and extensive enough for air and exercise and lodged in barracks as roomy and good as are provided by the party in whose power they are for its own troops. But if any officer shall break his parole by leaving the district so assigned him, or any other prisoner shall escape from the limits of his cantonment after they shall have been designated to him, such individual, officer, or other prisoner, shall forfeit so much of the benefit of this article as provides for his liberty on parole or in cantonment. And if any officer so breaking his parole or any common soldier so escaping from the limits assigned him, shall afterwards be found in arms previously to his being regularly exchanged, the person so offending shall be dealt with according to the established laws of war. The officers shall be daily furnished, by the

party in whose power they are, with as many rations, and of the same articles, as are allowed either in kind or by commutation, to officers of equal rank in its own army; and all others shall be daily furnished with such ration as is allowed to a common soldier in its own service; the value of all which supplies shall, at the close of the war, or at periods to be agreed upon between the respective commanders, be paid by the other party, on a mutual adjustment of accounts for the subsistence of prisoners; and such accounts shall not be mingled with or set off against any others, nor the balance due on them withheld, as a compensation or reprisal for any cause whatever, real or pretended. Each party shall be allowed to keep a commissary of prisoners, appointed by itself, with every cantonment of prisoners, in possession of the other; which commissary shall see the prisoners as often as he pleases; shall be allowed to receive, exempt from all duties and taxes, and to distribute, whatever comforts may be sent to them by their friends; and shall be free to transmit his reports in open letters to the party by whom he is employed. And it is declared that neither the pretense that war dissolves all treaties, nor any other whatever, shall be considered as annulling or suspending the solemn covenant contained in this article. On the contrary, the state of war is precisely that for which it is provided; and, during which, its stipulations are to be as sacredly observed as the most acknowledged obligations under the law of nature or nations.

Article XXIII

This treaty shall be ratified by the President of the United States of America, by and with the advice and consent of the Senate thereof; and by the President of the Mexican Republic, with the previous approbation of its general Congress; and the ratifications shall be exchanged in the City of Washington, or at the seat of Government of Mexico, in four months from the date of the signature hereof, or sooner if practicable. In faith whereof we, the respective Plenipotentiaries, have signed this treaty of peace, friendship, limits, and settlement, and have hereunto affixed our seals respectively. Done in quintuplicate, at the city of Guadalupe Hidalgo, on the second day of February, in the year of our Lord one thousand eight hundred and forty-eight.

N. P. TRIST
LUIS P. CUEVAS
BERNARDO COUTO
MIGL. ATRISTAIN

LESSON NINE

THE WESTERN MEXICO TREATY

Gadsden Purchase Treaty

(December 30, 1853)

United States Congress

The History[9]

The Gadsden Purchase, or Treaty, was an agreement between the United States and Mexico, finalized in 1854, in which the United States agreed to pay Mexico $10 million for a 29,670 square mile portion of Mexico that later became part of Arizona and New Mexico. Gadsden's Purchase provided the land necessary for a southern transcontinental railroad and attempted to resolve conflicts that lingered after the Mexican-American War.

While the Treaty of Guadalupe Hidalgo formally ended the Mexican-American War in February 1848, tensions between the Governments of Mexico and the United States continued to simmer over the next six years. The two countries each claimed the Mesilla Valley as part of their own country. The Mexican Government demanded monetary compensation for Native American attacks in the region because, under the Treaty, the United States had agreed to protect Mexico from such attacks; however, the United States refused to comply, insisting that while they had agreed to protect Mexico from Native American attacks, they had not agreed to financially compensate for attacks that did occur. The persistent efforts of private American citizens to enter Mexico illegally and incite rebellions in an effort to gain territory exacerbated tensions between the governments.

These continuing tensions between Mexico and the United States complicated U.S. efforts to find a southern route for a transcontinental railroad as the only viable routes passed through Mexican territory. In 1847, the United States attempted to buy the Isthmus of Tehuantepec, an isthmus on the southern edge of North America, as an alternative means of providing a southern connection between the Atlantic and Pacific oceans. Mexico, however, had already granted Mexican Don José de Garay the right to build colonies for Americans on the isthmus with capital from the New Orleans Company. Fearing the colonists would rebel as those in Texas had, Mexican President Juan Ceballos revoked the grant, angering U.S. investors.

In 1853, Mexican officials evicted Americans from their property in the disputed Mesilla Valley. When the U.S. Government did not act, Governor William Lane of New Mexico declared the Mesilla Valley part of the U.S. territory of New Mexico. Mexican President Antonio de Santa Anna responded by sending troops into the valley. Attempting to defuse the situation, U.S.

---

[9] Originally published as "Diplomacy and Westward Expansion: Gadsden Purchase (1853–1854)," *Timeline of U.S. Diplomatic History (1830–1860)*, Office of the Historian, Bureau of Public Affairs, U.S. Department of State, Washington, DC, 2000. For additional information see "Diplomacy and Westward Expansion: Gadsden Purchase (1853–1854)," *Timeline of U.S. Diplomatic History (1830–1860)*, Office of the Historian, Bureau of Public Affairs, U.S. Department of State, Washington, DC, 2004. This agency is listed in the *National Resource Directory* section of this volume.

President Franklin Pierce sent James Gadsden, the new U.S. Minister to Mexico, to negotiate with Santa Anna. Secretary of State William Marcy instructed Gadsden to renegotiate a border that provided a route for a southern railroad, arrange for a release of U.S. financial obligations for Native American attacks, and settle the monetary claims between the countries related to the Garay project.

Gadsden met with Santa Anna on September 25, 1853. President Pierce sent verbal instructions for Gadsden through Christopher Ward, an agent for U.S. investors in the Garay project, giving Gadsden negotiating options ranging from $50 million for lower California and a large portion of northern Mexico to $15 million for a smaller land deal that would still provide for a southern railroad. Ward also lied to Gadsden, stating the President wanted the claims of the Garay party addressed in any treaty concluded with the Mexican Government; however, President Pierce never gave Ward these instructions because he did not believe in government involvement in affairs between private companies and foreign governments.

Santa Anna refused to sell a large portion of Mexico, but he needed money to fund an army to put down ongoing rebellions, so on December 30, 1853 he and Gadsden signed a treaty stipulating that the United States would pay $15 million for 45,000 square miles south of the New Mexico territory and assume private American claims, including those related to the Garay deal. The United States Government agreed to work toward preventing American raids along Mexico's border and Mexico voided U.S. responsibility for Native American attacks.

With a great deal of difficulty resulting from the increasing strife between the northern and southern states, the U.S. Senate ratified a revised treaty on April 25, 1854. The new treaty reduced the amount paid to Mexico to $10 million and the land purchased to 29,670 square miles, and removed any mention of Native American attacks and private claims. President Pierce signed the treaty and Gadsden presented the new treaty to Santa Anna, who signed it on June 8, 1854.

After Gadsden's Purchase a new border dispute caused tension over the United States' payment, and the treaty failed to resolve the issues surrounding financial claims and border attacks. However, it did create the southern border of the present-day United States, despite the beliefs of the vast majority of policymakers at the time who thought the United States would eventually expand further into Mexico.

The Document

Gadsden Purchase Treaty

WHEREAS a treaty between the United States of America and the Mexican Republic was concluded and signed at the City of Mexico on the thirtieth day of December, one thousand eight hundred and fifty-three; which treaty, as amended by the Senate of the United States, and being in the English and Spanish languages, is word for word as follows:

In the Name of Almighty God:

The Republic of Mexico and the United States of America desiring to remove every cause of disagreement which might interfere in any manner with the better friendship and intercourse between the two countries, and especially in respect to the true limits which should be established, when, notwithstanding what was covenanted in the treaty of Guadalupe Hidalgo in the year 1848, opposite interpretations have been urged, which might give occasion to questions of serious moment: to avoid these, and to strengthen and more firmly maintain the peace which happily prevails between the two republics, the President of the United States has, for this purpose, appointed James Gadsden, Envoy Extraordinary and Minister Plenipotentiary of the same, near the Mexican government, and the President of Mexico has appointed as Plenipotentiary "ad hoc" his excellency Don Manuel Diez de Bonilla, cavalier grand cross of the national and distinguished order of Guadalupe, and Secretary of State, and of the office of Foreign Relations, and Don Jose Salazar Ylarregui and General Mariano Monterde as scientific commissioners, invested with full powers for this negotiation, who, having communicated their respective full powers, and finding them in due and proper form, have agreed upon the articles following:

ARTICLE I.

The Mexican Republic agrees to designate the following as her true limits with the United States for the future: retaining the same dividing line between the two Californias as already defined and established, according to the 5th article of the treaty of Guadalupe Hidalgo, the limits between the two republics shall be as follows: Beginning in the Gulf of Mexico, three leagues from land, opposite the mouth of the Rio Grande, as provided in the 5th article of the treaty of Guadalupe Hidalgo; thence, as defined in the said article, up the middle of that river to the point where the parallel of 31° 47' north latitude crosses the same; thence due west one hundred miles; thence south to the parallel of 31° 20' north latitude; thence along the said parallel of 31° 20' to the 111th meridian of longitude west of Greenwich; thence in a straight line to a point on the Colorado River twenty English miles below the junction of the Gila and Colorado rivers; thence up the middle of the said river Colorado until it intersects the present line between the United States and Mexico.

For the performance of this portion of the treaty, each of the two governments shall nominate one commissioner, to the end that, by common consent the two thus nominated, having met in the city of Paso del Norte, three months after the exchange of the ratifications of this treaty, may proceed to survey and mark out upon the land the dividing line stipulated by this article, where it shall not have already been surveyed and established by the mixed commission, according to the treaty of Guadalupe, keeping a journal and making proper plans of their operations. For this purpose, if they should judge it necessary, the contracting parties shall be at liberty each to unite to its respective commissioner, scientific or other assistants, such as astronomers and surveyors, whose concurrence shall not be considered necessary for the settlement and of a true line of division between the two Republics; that line shall be alone established upon which the commissioners may fix, their consent in this particular being considered decisive and an integral part of this treaty, without necessity of ulterior ratification or approval, and without room for interpretation of any kind by either of the parties contracting.

The dividing line thus established shall, in all time, be faithfully respected by the two governments, without any variation therein, unless of the express and free consent of the two, given in conformity to the principles of the law of nations, and in accordance with the constitution of each country respectively.

In consequence, the stipulation in the 5th article of the treaty of Guadalupe Hidalgo upon the boundary line therein described is no longer of any force, wherein it may conflict with that here established, the said line being considered annulled and abolished wherever it may not coincide with the present, and in the same manner remaining in full force where in accordance with the same.

ARTICLE II.

The government of Mexico hereby releases the United States from all liability on account of the obligations contained in the eleventh article of the treaty of Guadalupe Hidalgo; and the said article and the thirty-third article of the treaty of amity, commerce, and navigation between the United States of America and the United Mexican States concluded at Mexico, on the fifth day of April, 1831, are hereby abrogated.

ARTICLE III.

In consideration of the foregoing stipulations, the Government of the United States agrees to pay to the government of Mexico, in the city of New York, the sum of ten millions of dollars, of which seven millions shall be paid immediately upon the exchange of the ratifications of this treaty, and the remaining three millions as soon as the boundary line shall be surveyed, marked, and established.

ARTICLE IV.

The provisions of the 6th and 7th articles of the treaty of Guadalupe Hidalgo having been rendered nugatory, for the most part, by the cession of territory granted in the first article of this treaty, the said articles are hereby abrogated and annulled, and the provisions as herein expressed substituted therefor. The vessels, and citizens of the United States shall, in all time, have free and uninterrupted passage through the Gulf of California, to and from their possessions situated north of the boundary line of the two countries. It being understood that this passage is to be by navigating the Gulf of California and the river Colorado, and not by land, without the express consent of the Mexican government; and precisely the same provisions, stipulations, and restrictions, in all respects, are hereby agreed upon and adopted, and shall be scrupulously observed and enforced by the two contracting governments in reference to the Rio Colorado, so far and for such distance as the middle of that river is made their common boundary line by the first article of this treaty.

The several provisions, stipulations, and restrictions contained in the 7th article of the treaty of Guadalupe Hidalgo shall remain in force only so far as regards the Rio Bravo del Forte, below the initial of the said boundary provided in the first article of this treaty; that is to say, below the intersection of the 31° 47' 30" parallel of latitude, with the boundary line established by the late treaty dividing said river from its mouth upwards, according to the fifth article of the treaty of Guadalupe.

ARTICLE V.

All the provisions of the eighth and ninth, sixteenth and seventeenth articles of the treaty of Guadalupe Hidalgo, shall apply to the territory ceded by the Mexican Republic in the first article of the present treaty, and to all the rights of persons and property, both civil and ecclesiastical, within the same, as fully and as effectually as if the said articles were herein again recited and set forth.

ARTICLE VI.

No grants of land within the territory ceded by the first article of this treaty bearing date subsequent to the day – twenty-fifth of September – when the minister and subscriber to this treaty on the part of the United States, proposed to the Government of Mexico to terminate the question of boundary, will be considered valid or be recognized by the United States, or will any grants made previously be respected or be considered as obligatory which have not been located and duly recorded in the archives of Mexico.

ARTICLE VII.

Should there at any future period (which God forbid) occur any disagreement between the two nations which might lead to a rupture of their relations and reciprocal peace, they bind themselves in like manner to procure by every possible method the adjustment of every difference; and should they still in this manner not succeed, never will they proceed to a declaration of war, without having previously paid attention to what has been set forth in article twenty-one of the treaty of Guadalupe for similar cases; which article, as well as the twenty-second is here reaffirmed.

ARTICLE VIII.

The Mexican Government having on the 5th of February, 1853, authorized the early construction of a plank and railroad across the Isthmus of Tehuantepec, and, to secure the stable benefits of said transit way to the persons and merchandise of the citizens of Mexico and the United States, it is stipulated that neither government will interpose any obstacle to the transit of persons and merchandise of both nations; and at no time shall higher charges be made on the transit of persons and property of citizens of the United States, than may be made on the persons and property of other foreign nations, nor shall any interest in said transit way, nor in the proceeds thereof, be transferred to any foreign government.

The United States, by its agents, shall have the right to transport across the isthmus, in closed bags, the mails of the United States not intended for distribution along the line of communication; also the effects of the United States government and its citizens, which may be intended for transit, and not for distribution on the isthmus, free of custom-house or other charges by the Mexican government. Neither passports nor letters of security will be required of persons crossing the isthmus and not remaining in the country.

When the construction of the railroad shall be completed, the Mexican government agrees to open a port of entry in addition to the port of Vera Cruz, at or near the terminus of said road on the Gulf of Mexico.

The two governments will enter into arrangements for the prompt transit of troops and munitions of the United States, which that government may have occasion to send from one part of its territory to another, lying on opposite sides of the continent.

The Mexican government having agreed to protect with its whole power the prosecution, preservation, and security of the work, the United States may extend its protection as it shall judge wise to it when it may feel sanctioned and warranted by the public or international law.

ARTICLE IX.

This treaty shall be ratified, and the respective ratifications shall be exchanged at the city of Washington within the exact period of six months from the date of its signature, or sooner, if possible.

In testimony whereof, we, the plenipotentiaries of the contracting parties, have hereunto affixed our hands and seals at Mexico, the thirtieth (30th) day of December, in the year of our Lord one thousand eight hundred and fifty-three, in the thirty-third year of the independence of the Mexican republic, and the seventy-eighth of that of the United States.

JAMES GADSDEN,
MANUEL DIEZ DE BONILLA
JOSE SALAZAR YLARBEGUI
J. MARIANO MONTERDE,

And whereas the said treaty, as amended, has been duly ratified on both parts, and the respective ratifications of the same have this day been exchanged at Washington, by WILLIAM L. MARCY, Secretary of State of the United States, and SENOR GENERAL DON JUAN N. ALMONTE, Envoy Extraordinary and Minister Plenipotentiary of the Mexican Republic, on the part of their respective Governments:

Now, therefore, be it known that I, FRANKLIN PIERCE, President of the United States of America, have caused the said treaty to be made public, to the end that the same, and every clause and article thereof, may be observed and fulfilled with good faith by the United States and the citizens thereof

In witness whereof I have hereunto set my hand and caused the seal of the United States to be affixed.

Done at the city of Washington, this thirtieth day of June, in the year of our Lord one thousand eight hundred and fifty-four, and of the Independence of the United States the seventy-eighth.

BY THE PRESIDENT:
FRANKLIN PIERCE,
W. L. MARCY, Secretary of State.

LESSON TEN

THE ALASKA TREATY

Alaska Treaty

(March 30, 1867)

United States Congress

The History[10]

In 1866 the Russian government offered to sell the territory of Alaska to the United States. Secretary of State William H. Seward, enthusiastic about the prospects of American expansion, negotiated the deal for the Americans. Edward de Stoeckl, Russian minister to the United States, negotiated for the Russians. On March 30, 1867, the two parties agreed that the United States would pay Russia $7.2 million for the territory of Alaska.

For less than 2 cents an acre, the United States acquired nearly 600,000 square miles. Opponents of the Alaska Purchase persisted in calling it "Seward's Folly" or "Seward's Icebox" until 1896, when the great Klondike Gold Strike convinced even the harshest critics that Alaska was a valuable addition to American territory.

The check for $7.2 million was made payable to the Russian Minister to the United States Edward de Stoeckl, who negotiated the deal for the Russians. Also shown here is the Treaty of Cession, signed by Tzar Alexander II, which formally concluded the agreement for the purchase of Alaska from Russia.

Juneau officially replaced Sitka as capital in 1900, but it did not begin to function as such until 1906. In the same year Alaska was finally awarded a territorial representative in Congress. A new era began for Alaska when local government was established in 1912 and it became a U.S. territory. The building of the Alaska railroad from Seward to Fairbanks was commenced with government funds in 1915. Already, however, gold mining was dying out, and Alaska receded into one of its quiet periods. The fishing industry, which had gradually advanced during the gold era, became the major enterprise.

Alaska enjoyed an economic boom during World War II. The Alaska Highway was built, supplying a weak but much-needed link with the United States. After Japanese troops occupied the Aleutian islands of Attu and Kiska, U.S. forces prepared for a counterattack. Attu was retaken in May 1943, after intense fighting, and the Japanese evacuated Kiska in August after intensive U.S. bombardments. Dutch Harbor became a major key in the U.S. defense system. The growth of air travel after the war and the permanent military bases established in Alaska resulted in tremendous growth; between 1950 and 1960 the population nearly doubled.

---

[10] Originally published as "Check for the Purchase of Alaska (1868)," *100 Milestone Documents*, The National Archives, U.S. National Archives and Records Administration, College Park, Maryland, 2008. For additional information see "The Purchase of Alaska (1868)," *America's Historical Documents*, U.S. National Archives and Records Administration, College Park, Maryland, 2008. This agency is listed in the *National Resource Directory* section of this volume.

In 1958, Alaskans approved statehood by a 5 to 1 vote, and on January 3, 1959, Alaska was officially admitted into the Union as a state, the first since Arizona in 1912. On March 27,1964, the strongest earthquake ever recorded in North America occurred in Alaska, taking approximately 114 lives and causing extensive property damage. Some cities were almost totally destroyed, and the fishing industry was especially hard hit, with the loss of fleets, docks, and canneries from the resulting tsunami. Reconstruction, with large-scale federal aid, was rapid. The Alaska Native Claims Settlement Act (1971) gave roughly 44 million acres (17.8 million hectares; 10% of the state) and almost $1 billion to Alaskan native peoples in exchange for renunciation of all aboriginal claims to land in the state.

The Document

Alaska Purchase Treaty[1]

Whereas a treaty between the United States of America and his Majesty the Emperor of all the Russias was concluded and signed by their respective plenipotentiaries at the city of Washington, on the thirtieth day of March, last, which treaty, being in English and French languages, is, word for word as follows:

(The French version is omitted for brevity).

The United States of America and His Majesty the Emperor of all the Russias, being desirous of strengthening, if possible, the good understanding which exists between them, have, for that purpose, appointed as their Plenipotentiaries: the President of the United States, William H. Seward, Secretary of State; and His Majesty the Emperor of all the Russias, the Privy Councillor Edward de Stoeckl, his Envoy Extraordinary and Minister Plenipotentiary to the United States.

And the said Plenipotentiaries, having exchanged their full powers, which were found to be in due form, have agreed upon and signed the following articles:

ARTICLE I.

His Majesty the Emperor of all the Russias agrees to cede to the United States, by this convention, immediately upon the exchange of the ratifications thereof, all the territory and dominion now possessed by his said Majesty on the continent of America and in the adjacent islands, the same being contained within the geographical limits herein set forth, to wit: The eastern limit is the line of demarcation between the Russian and the British possessions in North America, as established by the convention between Russia and Great Britain, of February 28-16, 1825, and described in Articles III and IV of said convention, in the following terms:

> "Commencing from the southernmost point of the island called Prince of Wales Island, which point lies in the parallel of 54 degrees 40 minutes north latitude, and between the 131st and the 133d degree of west longitude, (meridian of Greenwich,) the said line shall ascend to the north along the channel called

Portland channel, as far as the point of the continent where it strikes the 56th degree of north latitude; from this last-mentioned point, the line of demarcation shall follow the summit of the mountains situated parallel to the coast as far as the point of intersection of the 141st degree of west longitude, (of the same meridian;) and finally, from the said point of intersection, the said meridian line of the 141st degree, in its prolongation as far as the Frozen ocean. "IV. With reference to the line of demarcation laid down in the preceding article, it is understood –

"1st. That the island called Prince of Wales Island shall belong wholly to Russia," (now, by this cession, to the United States.)

"2d. That whenever the summit of the mountains which extend in a direction parallel to the coast from the 56th degree of north latitude to the point of intersection of the 141st degree of west longitude shall prove to be at the distance of more than ten marine leagues from the ocean, the limit between the British possessions and the line of coast which is to belong to Russia as above mentioned (that is to say, the limit to the possessions ceded by this convention) shall be formed by a line parallel to the winding of the coast, and which shall never exceed the distance of ten marine leagues therefrom."

The western limit within which the territories and dominion conveyed, are contained, passes through a point in Behring's straits on the parallel of sixty-five degrees thirty minutes north latitude, at its intersection by the meridian which passes midway between the islands of Krusenstern, or Ignalook, and the island of Ratmanoff, or Noonarbook, and proceeds due north, without limitation, into the same Frozen ocean. The same western limit, beginning at the same initial point, proceeds thence in a course nearly southwest through Behring's straits and Behring's sea, so as to pass midway between the northwest point of the island of St. Lawrence and the southeast point of Cape Choukotski, to the meridian of one hundred and seventy-two west longitude; thence, from the intersection of that meridian, in a south-westerly direction, so as to pass midway between the island of Attou and the Copper island of the Kormandorski couplet or group in the North Pacific ocean, to the meridian of one hundred and ninety-three degrees west longitude, so as to include in the territory conveyed the whole of the Aleutian islands east of that meridian.

ARTICLE II.

In the cession of territory and dominion made by the preceding article are included the right of property in all public lots and squares, vacant lands, and all public buildings, fortifications, barracks, and other edifices which are not private individual property. It is, however, understood and agreed, that the churches which have been built in the ceded territory by the Russian government, shall remain the property of such members of the Greek Oriental Church resident in the territory, as may choose to worship therein. Any government archives, papers, and documents relative to the territory and dominion aforesaid, which may be now existing there, will be left in the possession of the agent of the United States; but an authenticated copy of such of them as may be required, will be, at all times, given by the United States to the Russian government, or to such Russian officers or subjects as they may apply for.

ARTICLE III.

The inhabitants of the ceded territory, according to their choice, reserving their natural allegiance, may return to Russia within three years; but if they should prefer to remain in the ceded territory, they, with the exception of uncivilized native tribes, shall be admitted to the enjoyment of all the rights, advantages, and immunities of citizens of the United States, and shall be maintained and protected in the free enjoyment of their liberty, property, and religion. The uncivilized tribes will be subject to such laws and regulations as the United States may, from time to time, adopt in regard to aboriginal tribes of that country.

ARTICLE IV.

His Majesty the Emperor of all the Russias shall appoint, with convenient despatch, an agent or agents for the purpose of formally delivering to a similar agent or agents appointed on behalf of the United States, the territory, dominion, property, dependencies and appurtenances which are ceded as above, and for doing any other act which may be necessary in regard thereto. But the cession, with the right of immediate possession, is nevertheless to be deemed complete and absolute on the exchange of ratifications, without waiting for such formal delivery.

ARTICLE V.

Immediately after the exchange of the ratifications of this convention, any fortifications or military posts which may be in the ceded territory shall be delivered to the agent of the United States, and any Russian troops which may be in the territory shall be withdrawn as soon as may be reasonably and conveniently practicable.

ARTICLE VI.

In consideration of the cession aforesaid, the United States agree to pay at the treasury in Washington, within ten months after the exchange of the ratifications of this convention, to the diplomatic representative or other agent of his Majesty the Emperor of all the Russias, duly authorized to receive the same, seven million two hundred thousand dollars in gold. The cession of territory and dominion herein made is hereby declared to be free and unencumbered by any reservations, privileges, franchises, grants, or possessions, by any associated companies, whether corporate or incorporate, Russian or any other, or by any parties, except merely private individual property holders; and the cession hereby made, conveys all the rights, franchises, and privileges now belonging to Russia in the said territory or dominion, and appurtenances thereto.

Article VII.

When this convention shall have been duly ratified by the President of the United States, by and with the advice and consent of the Senate, on the one part, and on the other by his Majesty the Emperor of all the Russias, the ratifications shall be exchanged at Washington within three months from the date hereof, or sooner if possible.

In faith whereof, the respective plenipotentiaries have signed this convention, and thereto affixed the seals of their arms.

Done at Washington, the thirtieth day of March, in the year of our Lord one thousand eight hundred and sixty-seven.

[L. S.] WILLIAM H. SEWARD.
[L. S.] EDOUARD DE STOECKL.

And whereas the said Treaty has been duly ratified on both parts, and the respective ratifications of the same were exchanged at Washington on this twentieth day of June, by William H. Seward, Secretary of State of the United States, and the Privy Counsellor Edward de Stoeckl, the Envoy Extraordinary of His Majesty the Emperor of all the Russias, on the part of their respective governments, Now, therefore, be it known that I, Andrew Johnson, President of the United States of America, have caused the said Treaty to be made public, to the end that the same and every clause and article thereof may be observed and fulfilled with good faith by the United States and the citizens thereof.

In witness whereof, I have hereunto set my hand, and caused the seal of the United States to be affixed.

Done at the city of Washington, this twentieth day of June in the year of our Lord one thousand eight hundred and sixty-seven, and of the Independence of the United States the ninety-first.

[L.S.] ANDREW JOHNSON
By the President:
William H. Seward, Secretary of State

Note

1. *Treaty concerning the Cession of the Russian Possessions in North America by his Majesty the Emperor of all the Russias to the United States of America; Concluded March 30, 1867; Ratified by the United States May 28, 1867; Exchanged June 20, 1867; Proclaimed by the United States June 20, 1867.*

LESSON ELEVEN

THE HAWAIIAN ISLAND ANNEXATION RESOLUTION

Hawaii Resolution

(July 7, 1898)

United States Congress

The History[11]

When the Hawaiian islands were formally annexed by the United States in 1898, the event marked the end of a lengthy internal struggle between native Hawaiians and white American businessmen for control of the Hawaiian government. In 1893 the last monarch of Hawaii, Queen Lili'uokalani, was overthrown by party of businessmen, who then imposed a provisional government. Soon after, President Benjamin Harrison submitted a treaty to annex the Hawaiian islands to the U.S. Senate for ratification. In 1897, the treaty effort was blocked when the newly-formed Hawaiian Patriotic League, composed of native Hawaiians, successfully petitioned the U.S. Congress in opposition to the treaty. The League's lobbying efforts left only 46 Senators in favor of the resolution, less than the ⅔ majority needed for approval of a treaty. The League's victory was short-lived, however, as unfolding world events soon forced the annexation issue to the fore again. With the explosion of the U.S.S. *Maine* in February 1898 signaling the start of the Spanish-American War, establishing a mid–Pacific fueling station and naval base became a strategic imperative for the United States. The Hawaiian islands were the clear choice, and this time Congress moved to annex the Hawaiian islands by Joint Resolution, a process requiring only a simple majority in both houses of Congress. On July 12, 1898, the Joint Resolution passed and the Hawaiian islands were officially annexed by the United States.

The Hawaiian islands had a well-established culture and long history of self-governance when Captain James Cook, the first European explorer to set foot on Hawaii, landed in 1778. The influence of European and American settlers quickly began to alter traditional ways of life. Originally governed by individual chiefs or kings, the islands united under the rule of a single monarch, King Kamehameha, in 1795, less than two decades after Cook's arrival. Later the traditional Hawaiian monarchy was overthrown in favor of a constitutional monarchy. Eventually, the monarchy itself was abandoned in favor of a government elected by a small group of enfranchised voters, although the Hawaiian monarch was retained as the ceremonial head of the government. Even elements of daily life felt the social and economic impact of the white planters, missionaries and businessmen. The landholding system changed, and many aspects of traditional culture were prohibited including teaching the Hawaiian language and performing the native Hula dance.

---

[11] Originally published as "Teaching with Documents: The 1897 Petition Against the Annexation of Hawaii," *Educators and Students Report*, The National Archives, U.S. National Archives and Records Administration, College Park, Maryland, 2008. For additional information see "Joint Resolution to Provide for Annexing the Hawaiian Islands to the United States (1868)," *100 Milestone Documents*, U.S. National Archives and Records Administration, College Park, Maryland, 2008. This agency is listed in the *National Resource Directory* section of this volume.

In 1887, the struggle for control of Hawaii was at its height as David Kalakaua was elected to the Hawaiian throne. King Kalakaua signed a reciprocity treaty with the United States making it possible for sugar to be sold to the U.S. market tax-free, but the *haole*– or "white" – businessmen were still distrustful of him. They criticized his ties to men they believed to be corrupt, his revival of Hawaiian traditions such as the historic Hula, and construction of the royal Iolani Palace. A scandal involving Kalakaua erupted in the very year he was crowned, and it united his opponents, a party of businessmen under the leadership of Lorrin Thurston. The opposition used the threat of violence to force Kalakaua to accept a new constitution that stripped the monarchy of executive powers and replaced the cabinet with members of the businessmen's party. The new constitution, which effectively disenfranchised most native Hawaiian voters, came to be known as the "Bayonet Constitution" because Kalakaua signed it under duress.

When King Kalakaua died in 1891, his sister Lili'uokalani succeeded him, and members of the native population persuaded the new queen to draft a new constitution in an attempt to restore native rights and powers. The move was countered by the Committee on Annexation, a small group of white businessmen and politicians who felt that annexation by the United States, the major importer of Hawaiian products, would be beneficial for the economy of Hawaii. Supported by John Stevens, the U.S. Minister to Hawaii, and a contingent of Marines from the warship, U.S.S. *Boston*, the Committee on Annexation overthrew Queen Lili'uokalani in a bloodless coup on January 17, 1893 and established a revolutionary regime.

Without permission from the U.S. State Department, Minister Stevens then recognized the new government and proclaimed Hawaii a U.S. protectorate. The Committee immediately proclaimed itself to be the Provisional Government. President Benjamin Harrison signed a treaty of annexation with the new government, but before the Senate could ratify it, Grover Cleveland replaced Harrison as president and subsequently withdrew the treaty.

Shortly into his presidency, Cleveland appointed James Blount as a special investigator to investigate the events in the Hawaiian islands. Blount found that Minister Stevens had acted improperly and ordered that the American flag be lowered from Hawaiian government buildings. He also ordered that Queen Lili'uokalani be restored to power, but Sanford Dole, the president of the Provisional Government of Hawaii, refused to turn over power. Dole successfully argued that the United States had no right to interfere in the internal affairs of Hawaii. The Provisional Government then proclaimed Hawaii a republic in 1894, and soon the Republic of Hawaii was officially recognized by the United States.

The overthrow of Lili'uokalani and imposition of the Republic of Hawaii was contrary to the will of the native Hawaiians. Native Hawaiians staged mass protest rallies and formed two gender-designated groups to protest the overthrow and prevent annexation. One was the *Hui Hawaii Aloha Aina*, loosely translated as the Hawaiian Patriotic League, and the other was its female counterpart, the *Hui Hawaii Aloha Aina o Na Wahine*. On January 5, 1895, the protests took the form of an armed attempt to derail the annexation but the armed revolt was suppressed by the forces of the Republic. The leaders of the revolt were imprisoned along with Queen Lili'uokalani who was jailed for failing to put down the revolt.

In March 1897, William McKinley was inaugurated as President of the United States.

McKinley was in favor of annexation, and the change in leadership was soon felt. On June 16, 1897, McKinley and three representatives of the government of the Republic of Hawaii – Lorrin Thurston, Francis Hatch, and William Kinney – signed a treaty of annexation. President McKinley then submitted the treaty to the U.S. Senate for ratification.

The *Hui Aloha Aina* for Women and the *Hui Aloha Aina* for Men now organized a mass petition drive. They hoped that if the U.S. government realized that the majority of native Hawaiian citizens opposed annexation, the move to annex Hawaii would be stopped. Between September 11 and October 2, 1897, the two groups collected petition signatures at public meetings held on each of the five principal islands of Hawaii. The petition, clearly marked "Petition Against Annexation" and written in both the Hawaiian and English languages, was signed by 21,269 native Hawaiian people, or more than half the 39,000 native Hawaiians and mixed-blood persons reported by the Hawaiian Commission census for the same year.

Four delegates, James Kaulia, David Kalauokalani, John Richardson, and William Auld, arrived in Washington, D.C. on December 6 with the 556-page petition in hand. That day, as they met with Queen Lili'uokalani, who was already in Washington lobbying against annexation, the second session of the 55th Congress opened. The delegates and Lili'uokalani planned a strategy to present the petition to the Senate.

The delegation and Lili'uokalani met Senator George Hoar, chairman of the Senate Committee on Foreign Relations on the following day, and on December 9, with the delegates present, Senator Hoar read the text of the petition to the Senate. It was formally accepted. The next day the delegates met with Secretary of State John Sherman and submitted a formal statement protesting the annexation to him. In the following days, the delegates met with many senators, voicing opposition to the annexation. By the time the delegates left Washington on February 27, 1898, there were only 46 senators willing to vote for annexation. The treaty was defeated in the Senate.

Other events brought the subject of annexation up again immediately. On February 15, 1898, the U.S. Battleship *Maine* was blown up in Havana harbor in Cuba. The ensuing Spanish-American War, part of which was fought in the Philippine Islands, established the strategic value of the Hawaiian islands as a mid-Pacific fueling station and naval installation. The pro-annexation forces in Congress submitted a proposal to annex the Hawaiian islands by joint resolution, which required only a simple majority vote in both houses. This eliminated the ⅔ majority needed to ratify a treaty, and by result, the necessary support in place. House Joint Resolution 259, 55th Congress, 2nd session, known as the "Newlands Resolution," passed Congress and was signed into law by President McKinley on July 7, 1898.

Once annexed by the United States, the Hawaiian islands remained a U.S. territory until 1959, when they were admitted to statehood as the 50th state. The story of the annexation is a story of conflicting goals as the white businessmen struggled to obtain favorable trade conditions and native Hawaiians sought to protect their cultural heritage and maintain a national identity. The 1897 Petition by the Hawaiian Patriotic League stands as evidence that the native Hawaiian people objected to annexation, but because the interests of the businessmen won out, over the coming decades most historians who wrote the history of Hawaii emphasized events as told by the Provisional Government and largely neglected the struggle of the Native Hawaiians. Today, there is a growing movement on the Islands to revive interest in the native Hawaiian language and culture. Primary sources such as this petition bear witness that there is another side to the story.

The Document

Hawaii Resolution[1]

To Provide for Annexing the Hawaiian Islands to the United States.

Whereas the Government of the Republic of Hawaii having, in due form, signified its consent, in the manner provided by its constitution, to cede absolutely and without reserve to the United States of America all rights of sovereignty of whatsoever kind in and over the Hawaiian Islands and their dependencies, and also to cede and transfer to the United States the absolute fee and ownership of all public, Government, or Crown lands, public buildings or edifices, ports, harbors, military equipment, and all other public property of every kind and description belonging to the Government of the Hawaiian Islands, together with every right and appurtenance thereunto appertaining; Therefore

Resolved by the Senate and House of Representatives of the United States of America in Congress Assembled, That said cession is accepted, ratified, and confirmed, and that the said Hawaiian Islands and their dependencies be, and they are hereby, annexed as a part of the territory of the United States and are subject to the sovereign dominion thereof, and that all and singular the property and rights hereinbefore mentioned are vested in the United States of America.

The existing laws of the United States relative to public lands shall not apply to such lands in the Hawaiian Islands; but the Congress of the United States shall enact special laws for their management and disposition: *Provided*, That all revenue from or proceeds of the same, except as regards such part thereof as may be used or occupied for the civil, military, or naval purposes of the United States, or may be assigned for the use of the local government, shall be used solely for the benefit of the inhabitants of the Hawaiian Islands for educational and other public purposes.

Until Congress shall provide for the government of such islands all the civil, judicial, and military powers exercised by the officers of the existing government in said islands shall be vested in such person or persons and shall be exercised in such manner as the President of the United States shall direct; and the President shall have the power to remove said officers and fill the vacancies so occasioned.

The existing treaties of the Hawaiian Islands with foreign nations shall forthwith cease and determine, being replaced by such treaties as may exist, or as may be hereafter concluded, between the United States and such foreign nations. The municipal legislation of the Hawaiian Islands, not enacted for the fulfillment of the treaties so extinguished, and not inconsistent with this joint resolution nor contrary to the Constitution of the United States nor to any existing treaty of the United States, shall remain in force until the Congress of the United States shall otherwise determine.

Until legislation shall be enacted extending the United States customs laws and regulations to the Hawaiian Islands the existing customs relations of the Hawaiian Islands with the United States and other countries shall remain unchanged.

The public debt of the Republic of Hawaii, lawfully existing at the date of the passage of this joint resolution, including the amounts due to depositors in the Hawaiian Postal Savings Bank, is hereby assumed by the Government of the United States; but the liability of the United States in this regard shall in no case exceed four million dollars. So long, however, as the existing Government and the present commercial relations of the Hawaiian Islands are continued as hereinbefore provided said Government shall continue to pay the interest on said debt.

There shall be no further immigration of Chinese into the Hawaiian Islands, except upon such conditions as are now or may hereafter be allowed by the laws of the United States; no Chinese, by reason of anything herein contained, shall be allowed to enter the United States from the Hawaiian Islands.

The President shall appoint five commissioners, at least two of whom shall be residents of the Hawaiian Islands, who shall, as soon as reasonably practicable, recommend to Congress such legislation concerning the Hawaiian Islands as they shall deem necessary or proper.

SEC. 2. That the commissioners hereinbefore provided for shall be appointed by the President, by and with the advice and consent of the Senate.

SEC. 3. That the sum of one hundred thousand dollars, or so much thereof as may be necessary; is hereby appropriated, out of any money in the Treasury not otherwise appropriated, and to be immediately available, to be expended at the discretion of the President of the United States of America, for the purpose of carrying this joint resolution into effect.

SEREXO E. PAYNE,
Speaker of the House of Representatives
Pro Tempore.
GARRETT A. HOBART,
Vice-President of the United States and
President of the Senate.

Approved July 7th, 1898.

WILLIAM McKINLEY.
President

NOTE

1. This is Resolution No. 5, known as the "Newlands Resolution," 2nd Session, 55TH Congress, July 7, 1898. During the period between annexation and the establishment of Territorial government, June 14, 1900, the relations between Hawaii and the United States remained practically unchanged. The laws of Hawaii continued in force, and the constitution and laws of the United States in general did not extend to Hawaii, except as otherwise provided by the resolution.

THE FUTURE

The Future of Democracy

Robert M. Gates

Senator Warner is a special friend. He has introduced me to the United States Senate for confirmation four times. The first time was more than 20 years ago. And that dates us both. He is a great Virginian, a great American, and we will certainly all miss him when he brings his remarkable career in public service to a close next year.

I want to thank Justice Sandra Day O'Connor, one of the most distinguished jurists and public servants in America, for inviting me today. It was Justice O'Connor who administered my oath of office as Director of Central Intelligence in 1991. And last year we served together on the Baker-Hamilton Commission. Little did I know that my sojourn to Iraq a little over a year ago with the group would be only the first of many such visits for me.

Justice O'Connor and I share something else in common – a love of the College of William and Mary, where she is currently the chancellor. And of course, it was a special pleasure to see her four months ago when I had the honor of giving the commencement address at my alma mater. Attending college here in Williamsburg shaped my love of history and my belief that public service is a vital component of a working democracy – and of a meaningful life.

This setting is fitting for my topic today: a "realist's" view of promoting democracy abroad.

I had quite a reputation as a pessimist when I was in the intelligence business. A journalist once described me as the Eeyore of national security – able to find the darkest cloud in any silver lining. I used to joke that when an intelligence officer smelled the flowers, he'd look around for the coffin. Today, as one looks around the world – wars in Iraq and Afghanistan, an ambitious and fanatical theocracy in Iran, a nuclear North Korea, terrorism, and more – there would seem to be ample grounds to be gloomy.

But there is a different perspective if we step back and look at the world through a wider lens – a perspective that shows a dramatic growth in human freedom and democracy in just the time since this fall's college freshmen were born. Since 1989, hundreds of millions of people – from Eastern and Central Europe and the former Soviet Union, to South Africa, Afghanistan, Iraq, and elsewhere – have been liberated: they have left the darkness of despotism and walked into the bright sunshine of freedom.

Many have seized the opportunity, and freedom has prospered and strengthened; others liberated from the yoke of tyrannical

*This chapter is based on a speech given by Robert M. Gates at the *World Forum on the Future of Democracy* held in Williamsburg, VA, on September 17, 2007. The entire speech is available on the U.S. Department of Defense website (http://www.defenselink.mil/).

ideologies or dictators continue to struggle to fully realize the dream. At no time in history, though, has freedom come to so many in so short a time. And in every case, the United States, overtly or covertly, in large ways or small, played a role in their liberation.

Still, we Americans continue to wrestle with the appropriate role this country should play in advancing freedom and democracy in the world. It was a source of friction through the entire Cold War. In truth, it has been a persistent question for this country throughout our history: How should we incorporate America's democratic ideals and aspirations into our relations with the rest of the world? And in particular, when to, and whether to try to change the way other nations govern themselves? Should America's mission to make the world "safe for democracy," as Woodrow Wilson said, or, in the words of John Quincy Adams, should America be "the well-wisher of freedom and independence of all" but the "champion and indicator only of our own"?

During my time today, I'd like to put this question and its associated debates in some historical context – a context I hope might help inform the difficult policy choices our nation faces today.

Let me first speak to geography – this place we are in.

It is a strange quirk of history that a backwoods outpost in an unexplored corner of America would hold in it the seeds of a global movement toward liberty and self-governance – toward the democratic institutions that underpin the free nations of the world and give hope to countless people in many others.

So much of what defines America first took root here in Virginia along the banks of the James River. When you think about it, the initial impetus for these institutions owed as much to the struggle for survival as to anything else. The challenges were myriad: along with disease, hunger, and war, the settlers faced no small number of divisions and discord. Four hundred years removed from those early days, it is all too easy to forget about these stormy beginnings.

The revolution that brought about this nation was similarly chaotic. As my distinguished William and Mary classmate, the historian Joe Ellis, wrote in his book, *Founding Brothers*, "No one present at the start knew how it would turn out in the end. What in retrospect has the look of a foreordained unfolding of God's will was in reality an improvisational affair in which sheer chance, pure luck – both good and bad – and specific decisions made in the crucible of specific military and political crises determined the outcome." Ellis further wrote "the real drama of the American Revolution ... was its inherent messiness. This ... exciting but terrifying sense that all the major players had at the time – namely, that they were making it up as they went along, improvising on the edge of catastrophe." We would do well to be mindful of the turbulence of our own early history as we contemplate the challenges facing contemporary fledgling democracies struggling to find their footing.

When I retired from government in 1993, it seemed that the success and spread of democracy was inexorable, a foregone conclusion – that with the collapse of the Soviet Union, the evolution of political systems had reached, in the words of one scholar at the time, the "end of history." But the relative calm in the immediate aftermath of the Cold War served only to mask new threats to the security of democratic nations: ethnic conflicts, new genocides, the proliferation of weapons of mass destruction – especially by rogue states and, above all, a new, more formidable, and more malignant form of terrorism embraced by Islamic extremists.

These new threats, and in particular, the conflicts in Iraq and Afghanistan, and the wider challenge of dealing with radical jihadist movements since September 11th, once again have people talking about the competing impulses in U.S. foreign policy: realism versus idealism, freedom versus security, values versus interests.

This is not a new debate. Not long after winning our own independence, the U.S. was faced with how to respond to the French Revolution – an issue that consumed the politics of the country during the 1790s. The issue was whether to support the revolutionary government and its war against an alliance of European monarchies led by Great Britain. To many, like Thomas Jefferson, the French Revolution, with its stated ideals of liberty, equality, and fraternity, seemed a natural successor to our own. Jefferson wrote that "this ball of liberty, I believe most piously, is now so well in motion that it will roll round the globe."

John Adams and the Federalists, however, were just as adamantly opposed. They were appalled by the revolution's excesses and feared the spread of violent French radicalism to our shores. In fact, they accused the Jeffersonians of being "pimps of France," who "represented cutthroats who walk in rags." The Federalists mocked Jefferson for his rhetorical defense of freedom and equality across the Atlantic while he continued to own slaves. Adams and Alexander Hamilton were, in turn, accused of being crypto-monarchists.

It was left to President George Washington to resolve the matter. He had said that: "My best wishes are irresistibly excited whensoever, in any country, I see an oppressed nation unfurl the banners of freedom." But the European wars and, in particular, our estrangement from the British, had begun to disrupt the lives of ordinary Americans by impeding trade and causing riots and refugees. Washington, understanding the fragility of America's position at the time, adopted a neutrality policy towards France and would go on to make a peace treaty with Great Britain – sparking massive protests and accusations of selling out the spirit of 1776.

Consider the great historic irony: The United States had recently broken free of the British monarchy only with the help of an absolutist French king. Yet when France itself turned in the direction of popular rule and was confronted by Europe's monarchies, the United States took a pass and made amends with our old British foe.

In short, from our earliest days, America's leaders have struggled with "realistic" versus "idealistic" approaches to the international challenges facing us. The most successful leaders, starting with Washington, have steadfastly encouraged the spread of liberty, democracy, and human rights. At the same time, however, they have fashioned policies blending different approaches with different emphases in different places and different times.

Over the last century, we have allied with tyrants to defeat other tyrants. We have sustained diplomatic relations with governments even as we supported those attempting their overthrow.

We have at times made human rights the centerpiece of our national strategy even as we did business with some of the worst violators of human rights. We have worked with authoritarian governments to advance our own security interests even while urging them to reform.

We have used our military to eliminate governments seen as a threat to our national security, to undo aggression, to end ethnic slaughter, and to prevent chaos. In recent times, we have done this in Grenada, Panama, Kuwait, the Balkans, Haiti, Afghanistan, and Iraq. In the process, we have brought the possibility of democracy and freedom to tens of millions more who had been oppressed or were suffering.

To win and protect our own freedom, the United States has made common cause with countries that were far from free – from Louis XVI, to one of history's true monsters, Joseph Stalin. Without the one there is no American independence. Without the other, no end to the Third Reich. It is neither hypocrisy nor cynicism to believe fervently in freedom while adopting different approaches to advancing freedom at different times along the way – including temporarily making common cause with despots to defeat greater or more urgent threats to our freedom or interests.

The consuming goal for most of my professional life was containing the threat of the Soviet Union and seeing a Europe made whole and free. For most of the Cold War, the ideal surely seemed distant, even unreachable. One prominent columnist wrote in *Time* magazine in 1982 that "it would be wishful thinking to predict that international Communism someday will either self-destruct or so exhaust itself."

During that struggle, as for most of our history, inspiring presidential rhetoric about freedom, along with many firm stands for human rights and self-determination, had to coexist with often grubby compromises and marriages of convenience that were necessary to stave off the Evil Empire.

But the Western democracies – joined as the Atlantic Alliance – came together to get the big things right. The democracies' shared belief in political and economic freedom and religious tolerance was the glue that held us fast despite the many quarrels along the way.

President Bush said in his second inaugural address, "[I]t is the policy of the United States to seek and support the growth of democratic movements and institutions in every nation and culture, with the ultimate goal of ending tyranny in our world."

When we discuss openly our desire for democratic values to take hold across the globe, we are describing a world that may be many years or decades off. Though achievement of the ideal may be limited by time, space, resources, or human nature, we must not allow ourselves to discard or disparage the ideal itself. It is vital that we speak out about what we believe and let the world know where we stand. It is vital that we give hope and aid to those who seek freedom.

I still remember working on the advance team for President Ford when he attended the Helsinki conference in 1975. Many critics were opposed to America's participation, since they believed that the accords did little but ratify the Soviet Union's takings in Eastern and Central Europe. The treaty's provisions on human rights were disparaged as little more than window dressing. However, the conference and treaty represent another of history's ironies. The Soviets demanded the conference for decades, finally got it, and it helped destroy them from the inside. We "realists" opposed holding the conference for decades, and attended grudgingly. We were wrong. For the meeting played a key role in our winning the Cold War.

Why? Because the human-rights provisions of the treaty made a moral statement whose significance was not lost on the dissidents behind the Iron Curtain. Helsinki became a spur for action, a rallying cry to fight tyranny from within and plant democracy in its place.

Vaclav Havel later said that the accords were a "shield, a chance to resist coercion and make it more difficult for the forces of coercion to retaliate." Lech Walesa called it a turning point "on the road to change in Gdansk."

President Carter's promotion of the spirit of Helsinki – his elevation of human rights – for the first time in the Cold War denied the Soviet Union the respect and the legitimacy it craved. Ronald Reagan's muscular words – labeling the U.S.S.R. the "Evil Empire" and demanding that Mr. Gorbachev tear down that wall – combined with his muscular defense policies hastened the implosion of the Soviet system.

Did these policies reflect hard-edged realism or lofty idealism? Both, actually. Were they implemented to defend our interests or to spread our democratic values? Again, both.

An underlying theme of American history is that we are compelled to defend our security and our interests in ways that, in the long run, lead to the spread of democratic values and institutions.

Since September 11ᵗʰ, these questions, contradictions, and dilemmas have taken on new urgency and presented new challenges for decision-makers, especially in an information age where every flaw and inconsistency – in words or deeds – is highlighted, magnified, and disseminated around the globe.

And, as with the Cold War, every action we take sends a signal about the depth of our strength and resolve. For our friends and allies, as well as our enemies and potential adversaries, our commitment to democratic values must be matched by actions.

Consider Afghanistan. The democracies of the West and our partners are united in the desire to see stability and decent government take hold in a land that was not only Al Queda's base of operation, but also home to one of the most oppressive governments in the world. And yet, though there is little doubt about the justness, necessity, and legitimacy of the Afghanistan mission, even though we agree that democracy is key to enduring stability there, many Allies are reluctant to provide the necessary resources and put their men and women in the line of fire.

Afghanistan is, in a very real sense, a litmus test of whether an alliance of advanced democracies can still make sacrifices and meet commitments to advance democracy. It would be a mark of shame on all of us if an alliance built on the foundation of democratic values were to falter at the very moment that it tries to lay that foundation for democracy elsewhere – especially in a mission that is crucial to our own security.

Likewise, for America to leave Iraq and the Middle East in chaos would betray and demoralize our allies there and in the region, while emboldening our most dangerous adversaries. To abandon an Iraq where just two years ago 12 million people quite literally risked their lives to vote for a constitutional democracy would be an offense to our interests as well as our values, a setback for the cause of freedom as well as the goal of stability.

Americans have never been a patient people. Today, we look at Russia, China, Afghanistan, Iraq, and others – and wonder at their excruciatingly slow progress toward democratic institutions and the rule of law.

The eminent French historian Helene Carrere d'Encausse wrote in 1992: "Reforms, when they go against the political traditions of the centuries, cannot be imposed in a hurry merely by enshrining them in the law. It takes time, and generally they are accompanied by violence." She added: "Reforms that challenge centuries of social relations based on ... the exclusion of the majority of society from the political process, are too profound to be readily accepted by those who have to pay the price of reform, even if they are seen to be indispensible. Reforms need time to develop ... It is this time that reformers have often lacked."

For more than 60 years, from Germany and Japan to South Korea, the Balkans, Haiti, Afghanistan, and Iraq, we and our allies have provided reformers – those who seek a free and democratic society – with time for their efforts to take hold. We must be realists and recognize that the institutions that underpin an enduring free society can only take root over time.

It is our country's tragedy, and our glory, that the tender shoots of freedom around the world for so many decades have been so often nourished with American blood. The spread of liberty both manifests our ideals and protects our interests – in making the world "safe for democracy," we are also the "champion and vindicator" of our own. In reality, Wilson and Adams must coexist.

Throughout more than two centuries, the United States has made its share of mistakes. From time to time, we have strayed from our ideals and have been arrogant in dealing with others. Yet, what has brought us together with our democratic allies is a shared belief that the future of democracy and its spread is worth our enduring labors and sacrifices – reflecting both our interests and our ideals.

I would like to close by returning to this corner of Virginia. In September 1796, shortly before George Washington left office, he addressed in his farewell statement an American people who had passed through the dangerous fires of war and revolution to form a union that was far from "perfect," but was a historic accomplishment nonetheless. He told them: "You have, in common cause, fought and triumphed together; the independence and liberty you possess are the work of joint councils and joint efforts, of common dangers, sufferings, and successes."

In this historic place, among old friends and new, let us take time to reflect on the common causes in which we have fought and triumphed together – to protect our own liberty, and to extend its blessings to others. As we prepare for the challenges ahead, let us never forget that together we will face common dangers, sufferings, and successes – but with confidence that, together, we will continue to protect that tender shoot of liberty first planted in this place so long ago.

At the time this was written, Robert M. Gates was Secretary of Defense, Defense Department, U.S. Government, Washington, D.C. He was originally appointed by President Bush, and was asked to reman in this position by President Obama.

Civil Rights Act

(July 2, 1964)

United States Congress

▌The History[12]

In the 1960s, Americans who knew only the potential of "equal protection of the laws" expected by the president, the Congress, and the courts to fulfill the promise of the 14th Amendment. In response, all three branches of the federal government – as well as the public at large – debated a fundamental constitutional question: Does the Constitution's prohibition of denying equal protection always ban the use of racial, ethnic, or gender criteria in an attempt to bring social justice and social benefits?

In 1964 Congress passed Public Law 82352 (78 Stat. 241). The provisions of this civil rights act forbade discrimination on the basis of sex as well as race in hiring, promoting, and firing. The word "sex" was added at the last moment. According to the *West Encyclopedia of American Law*, Representative Howard W. Smith (D-VA) added the word. His critics argued that Smith, a conservative Southern opponent of federal civil rights, did so to kill the entire bill. Smith, however, argued that he had amended the bill in keeping with his support of Alice Paul and the National Women's Party with whom he had been working. Martha W. Griffiths (D-MI) led the effort to keep the word "sex" in the bill.

In the final legislation, Section 703 (a) made it unlawful for an employer to "fail or refuse to hire or to discharge any individual, or otherwise to discriminate against any individual with respect to his compensation, terms, conditions or privileges or employment, because of such individual's race, color, religion, sex, or national origin." The final bill also allowed sex to be a consideration when sex is a bona fide occupational qualification for the job. Title VII of the act created the Equal Employment Opportunity Commission (EEOC) to implement the law.

Subsequent legislation expanded the role of the EEOC. Today, according to the *U.S. Government Manual of 1998-99*, the EEOC enforces laws that prohibit discrimination based on race, color, religion, sex, national origin, disability, or age in hiring, promoting, firing, setting wages, testing, training, apprenticeship, and all other terms and conditions of employment. Race, color, sex, creed, and age are not protected classes. The proposal to add each group to

---

[12] Originally published as "Teaching With Documents: The Civil Rights Act of 1964 and the Equal Opportunity Employment Commission," *Educators and Students Report*, The National Archives, U.S. National Archives and Records Administration, College Park, Maryland, 2008. For additional information see "Teaching with Documents: The Civil Rights Act of 1964 and the Equal Employment Opportunity Commission," *Educators and Students Report*, U.S. National Archives and Records Administration, College Park, Maryland, 2008. This agency is listed in the *National Resource Directory* section of this volume.

protected-class status unleashed furious debate. But no words stimulate the passion of the debate more than "affirmative action."

As West defines the term, affirmative action "refers to both mandatory and voluntary programs intended to affirm the civil rights of designated classes of individuals by taking positive action to protect them" from discrimination. The issue for most Americans is fairness: Should the equal protection clause of the 14th Amendment be used to advance the liberty of one class of individuals for good reasons when that action may infringe on the liberty of another?

The EEOC, as an independent regulatory body, plays a major role in dealing with this issue. Since its creation in 1964, Congress has gradually extended EEOC powers to include investigatory authority, creating conciliation programs, filing lawsuits, and conducting voluntary assistance programs. While the Civil Rights Act of 1964 did not mention the words affirmative action, it did authorize the bureaucracy to make rules to help end discrimination. The EEOC has done so.

Today the regulatory authority of the EEOC includes enforcing a range of federal statutes prohibiting employment discrimination. According to the EEOC's own Web site, these include Title VII of the Civil Rights Act of 1964 that prohibits employment discrimination on the basis of race, color, religion, sex, or national origin; the Age Discrimination in Employment Act of 1967, and its amendments, that prohibits employment discrimination against individuals 40 years of age or older; the Equal Pay Act of 1963 that prohibits discrimination on the basis of gender in compensation for substantially similar work under similar conditions; Title I of the Americans with Disabilities Act of 1990 that prohibits employment discrimination on the basis of disability in both the public and private sector, excluding the federal government; the Civil Rights Act of 1991 that provides for monetary damages in case of intentional discrimination; and Section 501 of the Rehabilitation Act of 1973, as amended, that prohibits employment discrimination against federal employees with disabilities. Title IX of the Education Act of 1972 forbade gender discrimination in education programs, including athletics, that received federal dollars. In the late 1970s Congress passed the Pregnancy Discrimination Act. This made it illegal for employers to exclude pregnancy and childbirth from their sick leave and health benefits plans.

Presidents also weighed in, employing a series of executive orders. President Lyndon B. Johnson ordered all executive agencies to require federal contractors to "take affirmative action to ensure that applicants are employed and that employees are treated during employment without regard to race, color, religion, sex, or national origin." This marked the first use of the phrase "affirmative action." In 1969 an executive order required that every level of federal service offer equal opportunities for women and established a program to implement that action. President Richard Nixon's Department of Labor adopted a plan requiring federal contractors to assess their employees to identify gender and race and to set goals to end any under-representation of women and minorities. By the 1990s Democratic and Republican administrations had taken a variety of actions that resulted in 160 different affirmative action federal programs. State and local governments were following suit.

The courts also addressed affirmative action. In addition to dealing with race, color, creed, and age, from the 1970s forward, the court dealt with gender questions. It voided arbitrary weight and height requirements (*Dothard v. Rawlinson*), erased mandatory pregnancy leaves (*Cleveland*

Board of Education v. LaFleur), allowed public employers to use carefully constructed affirmative action plans to remedy specific past discrimination that resulted in women and minorities being under-represented in the workplace (*Johnson v. Transportation Agency, Santa Clara County*), and upheld state and local laws prohibiting gender discrimination.

By the late 1970s all branches of the federal government and most state governments had taken at least some action to fulfill the promise of equal protection under the law. The EEOC served as the agent of implementation and complaint. Its activism divided liberals and conservatives, illuminating their differing views about the proper scope of government. In general, the political liberals embraced the creation of the EEOC as the birth of a federal regulatory authority that could promote the goal of equality by designing policies to help the historically disadvantaged, including women and minorities. In contrast, political conservatives saw the EEOC as a violation of their belief in fewer government regulations and fewer federal policies. To them, creating a strong economy, free from government intervention, would produce gains that would benefit the historically disadvantaged. Even the nonideological segment of the American population asked: What should government do, if anything, to ensure equal protection under the law?

In fiscal year 1997, the EEOC collected $111 million dollars in financial benefits for people who filed claims of discrimination. Its recent successful efforts include a $34 million settlement in a sexual harassment case with Mitsubishi Motor Manufacturing of America, resulting in the company's adoption of changes to its sexual harassment prevention policy. Working with state and local programs, the EEOC processes 48,000 claims annually.

The Document

Civil Rights Act

To enforce the constitutional right to vote, to confer jurisdiction upon the district courts of the United States to provide injunctive relief against discrimination in public accommodations, to authorize the Attorney General to institute suits to protect constitutional rights in public facilities and public education, to extend the Commission on Civil Rights, to prevent discrimination in federally assisted programs, to establish a Commission on Equal Employment Opportunity, and for other purposes.

Be it enacted by the Senate and House of Representatives of the United States of America in Congress assembled, That this Act may be cited as the "Civil Rights Act of 1964."

TITLE I – VOTING RIGHTS

SEC. 101. Section 2004 of the Revised Statutes (42 U.S.C. 1971), as amended by section 131 of the Civil Rights Act of 1957 (71 Stat. 637), and as further amended by section 601 of the Civil Rights Act of 1960 (74 Stat. 90), is further amended as follows:

(a) Insert "1" after "(a)" in subsection (a) and add at the end of subsection (a) the following new paragraphs:

"(2) No person acting under color of law shall –

"(A) in determining whether any individual is qualified under State law or laws to vote in any Federal election, apply any standard, practice, or procedure different from the standards, practices, or procedures applied under such law or laws to other individuals within the same county, parish, or similar political subdivision who have been found by State officials to be qualified to vote;

"(B) deny the right of any individual to vote in any Federal election because of an error or omission on any record or paper relating to any application, registration, or other act requisite to voting, if such error or omission is not material in determining whether such individual is qualified under State law to vote in such election; or

"(C) employ any literacy test as a qualification for voting in any Federal election unless (i) such test is administered to each individual and is conducted wholly in writing, and (ii) a certified copy of the test and of the answers given by the individual is furnished to him within twenty-five days of the submission of his request made within the period of time during which records and papers are required to be retained and preserved pursuant to title III of the Civil Rights Act of 1960 (42 U.S.C. 1974 – 74e; 74 Stat. 88): Provided, however, That the Attorney General may enter into agreements with appropriate State or local authorities that preparation, conduct, and maintenance of such tests in accordance with the provisions of applicable State or local law, including such special provisions as are necessary in the preparation, conduct, and maintenance of such tests for persons who are blind or otherwise physically handicapped, meet the purposes of this subparagraph and constitute compliance therewith.

"(3) For purposes of this subsection –

"(A) the term 'vote' shall have the same meaning as in subsection (e) of this section;

"(B) the phrase 'literacy test' includes any test of the ability to read, write, understand, or interpret any matter."

(b) Insert immediately following the period at the end of the first sentence of subsection (c) the following new sentence: "If in any such proceeding literacy is a relevant fact there shall be a rebuttable presumption that any person who has not been adjudged an incompetent and who has completed the sixth grade in a public school in, or a private school accredited by, any State or territory, the District of Columbia, or the Commonwealth of Puerto Rico where instruction is carried on predominantly in the English language, possesses sufficient literacy, comprehension, and intelligence to vote in any Federal election."

(c) Add the following subsection "(f)" and designate the present subsection "(f)" as subsection "(g)": "(f) When used in subsection (a) or (c) of this section, the words 'Federal election' shall mean any general, special, or primary election held solely or in part for the purpose of electing or selecting any candidate for the office of President, Vice President, presidential elector, Member of the Senate, or Member of the House of Representatives."

(d) Add the following subsection "(h)":

"(h) In any proceeding instituted by the United States in any district court of the United States under this section in which the Attorney General requests a finding of a pattern or practice of discrimination pursuant to subsection (e) of this section the Attorney General, at the time he files the complaint, or any defendant in the proceeding, within twenty days after service upon him of the complaint, may file with the clerk of such court a request that a court of three judges be convened to hear and determine the entire case. A copy of the request for a three-judge court shall be immediately furnished by such clerk to the chief judge of the circuit (or in his absence, the presiding circuit judge of the circuit) in which the case is pending. Upon receipt of the copy of such request it shall be the duty of the chief justice of the circuit or the presiding circuit judge, as the case may be, to designate immediately three judges in such circuit, of whom at least one shall be a circuit judge and another of whom shall be a district judge of the court in which the proceeding was instituted, to hear and determine such case, and it shall be the duty of the judges so designated to assign the case for hearing at the earliest practicable date, to participate in the hearing and determination thereof, and to cause the case to be in every way expedited.

An appeal from the final judgment of such court will lie to the Supreme Court.

"In any proceeding brought under subsection (c) of this section to enforce subsection (b) of this section, or in the event neither the Attorney General nor any defendant files a request for a three-judge court in any proceeding authorized by this subsection, it shall be the duty of the chief judge of the district (or in his absence, the acting chief judge) in which the case is pending immediately to designate a judge in such district to hear and determine the case. In the event that no judge in the district is available to hear and determine the case, the chief judge of the district, or the acting chief judge, as the case may be, shall certify this fact to the chief judge of the circuit (or, in his absence, the acting chief judge) who shall then designate a district or circuit judge of the circuit to hear and determine the case.

"It shall be the duty of the judge designated pursuant to this section to assign the case for hearing at the earliest practicable date and to cause the case to be in every way expedited."

TITLE II – INJUNCTIVE RELIEF
AGAINST DISCRIMINATION IN PLACES OF PUBLIC ACCOMMODATION

SEC. 201. (a) All persons shall be entitled to the full and equal enjoyment of the goods, services, facilities, and privileges, advantages, and accommodations of any place of public accommodation, as defined in this section, without discrimination or segregation on the ground of race, color, religion, or national origin.

(b) Each of the following establishments which serves the public is a place of public accommodation within the meaning of this title if its operations affect commerce, or if discrimination or segregation by it is supported by State action:

(1) any inn, hotel, motel, or other establishment which provides lodging to transient guests, other than an establishment located within a building which contains not more than five rooms for rent or hire and which is actually occupied by the proprietor of such establishment as his residence;

(2) any restaurant, cafeteria, lunchroom, lunch counter, soda fountain, or other facility principally engaged in selling food for consumption on the premises, including, but not limited to, any such facility located on the premises of any retail establishment; or any gasoline station;

(3) any motion picture house, theater, concert hall, sports arena, stadium or other place of exhibition or entertainment; and

(4) any establishment (A)(i) which is physically located within the premises of any establishment otherwise covered by this subsection, or (ii) within the premises of which is physically located any such covered establishment, and (B) which holds itself out as serving patrons of such covered establishment.

(c) The operations of an establishment affect commerce within the meaning of this title if (1) it is one of the establishments described in paragraph (1) of subsection (b); (2) in the case of an establishment described in paragraph (2) of subsection (b), it serves or offers to serve interstate travelers or a substantial portion of the food which it serves, or gasoline or other products which it sells, has moved in commerce; (3) in the case of an establishment described in paragraph (3) of subsection (b), it customarily presents films, performances, athletic teams, exhibitions, or other sources of entertainment which move in commerce; and (4) in the case of an establishment described in paragraph (4) of subsection (b), it is physically located within the premises of, or there is physically located within its premises, an establishment the operations of which affect commerce within the meaning of this subsection. For purposes of this section, "commerce" means travel, trade, traffic, commerce, transportation, or communication among the several States, or between the District of Columbia and any State, or between any foreign country or any territory or possession and any State or the District of Columbia, or between points in the same State but through any other State or the District of Columbia or a foreign country.

(d) Discrimination or segregation by an establishment is supported by State action within the meaning of this title if such discrimination or segregation (1) is carried on under color of any law, statute, ordinance, or regulation; or (2) is carried on under color of any custom or usage required or enforced by officials of the State or political subdivision thereof; or (3) is required by action of the State or political subdivision thereof.

(e) The provisions of this title shall not apply to a private club or other establishment not in fact open to the public, except to the extent that the facilities of such establishment are made available to the customers or patrons of an establishment within the scope of subsection (b).

SEC. 202. All persons shall be entitled to be free, at any establishment or place, from discrimination or segregation of any kind on the ground of race, color, religion, or national origin, if such discrimination or segregation is or purports to be required by any law, statute, ordinance, regulation, rule, or order of a State or any agency or political subdivision thereof.

SEC. 203. No person shall (a) withhold, deny, or attempt to withhold or deny, or deprive or attempt to deprive, any person of any right or privilege secured by section 201 or 202, or (b) intimidate, threaten, or coerce, or attempt to intimidate, threaten, or coerce any person with the purpose of interfering with any right or privilege secured by section 201 or 202, or (c) punish or attempt to punish any person for exercising or attempting to exercise any right or privilege secured by section 201 or 202.

SEC. 204. (a) Whenever any person has engaged or there are reasonable grounds to believe that any person is about to engage in any act or practice prohibited by section 203, a civil action for preventive relief, including an application for a permanent or temporary injunction, restraining order, or other order, may be instituted by the person aggrieved and, upon timely application, the court may, in its discretion, permit the Attorney General to intervene in such civil action if he certifies that the case is of general public importance. Upon application by the complainant and in such circumstances as the court may deem just, the court may appoint an attorney for such complainant and may authorize the commencement of the civil action without the payment of fees, costs, or security.

(b) In any action commenced pursuant to this title, the court, in its discretion, may allow the prevailing party, other than the United States, a reasonable attorney's fee as part of the costs, and the United States shall be liable for costs the same as a private person.

(c) In the case of an alleged act or practice prohibited by this title which occurs in a State, or political subdivision of a State, which has a State or local law prohibiting such act or practice and establishing or authorizing a State or local authority to grant or seek relief from such practice or to institute criminal proceedings with respect thereto upon receiving notice thereof, no civil action may be brought under subsection (a) before the expiration of thirty days after written notice of such alleged act or practice has been given to the appropriate State or local authority by registered mail or in person, provided that the court may stay proceedings in such civil action pending the termination of State or local enforcement proceedings.

(d) In the case of an alleged act or practice prohibited by this title which occurs in a State, or political subdivision of a State, which has no State or local law prohibiting such act or practice, a civil action may be brought under subsection (a): Provided, That the court may refer the matter to the Community Relations Service established by title X of this Act for as long as the court believes there is a reasonable possibility of obtaining voluntary compliance, but for not more than sixty days: Provided further, That upon expiration of such sixty-day period, the court may extend such period for an additional period, not to exceed a cumulative total of one hundred and twenty days, if it believes there then exists a reasonable possibility of securing voluntary compliance.

SEC.205. The Service is authorized to make a full investigation of any complaint referred to it by the court under section 204(d) and may hold such hearings with respect thereto as may be necessary. The Service shall conduct any hearings with respect to any such complaint in executive session, and shall not release any testimony given therein except by agreement of all parties involved in the complaint with the permission of the court, and the Service shall endeavor to bring about a voluntary settlement between the parties.

SEC. 206. (a) Whenever the Attorney General has reasonable cause to believe that any person or group of persons is engaged in a pattern or practice of resistance to the full enjoyment of any of the rights secured by this title, and that the pattern or practice is of such a nature and is intended to deny the full exercise of the rights herein described, the Attorney General may bring a civil action in the appropriate district court of the United States by filing with it a complaint (1) signed by him (or in his absence the Acting Attorney General), (2) setting forth facts pertaining to such pattern or practice, and (3) requesting such preventive relief, including an application for a permanent or temporary injunction, restraining order or other order against the person or persons responsible for such pattern or practice, as he deems necessary to insure the full enjoyment of the rights herein described.

(b) In any such proceeding the Attorney General may file with the clerk of such court a request that a court of three judges be convened to hear and determine the case. Such request by the Attorney General shall be accompanied by a certificate that, in his opinion, the case is of general public importance. A copy of the certificate and request for a three-judge court shall be immediately furnished by such clerk to the chief judge of the circuit (or in his absence, the presiding circuit judge of the circuit) in which the case is pending. Upon receipt of the copy of such request it shall be the duty of the chief judge of the circuit or the presiding circuit judge, as the case may be, to designate immediately three judges in such circuit, of whom at least one shall be a circuit judge and another of whom shall be a district judge of the court in which the proceeding was instituted, to hear and determine such case, and it shall be the duty of the judges so designated to assign the case for hearing at the earliest practicable date, to participate in the hearing and determination thereof, and to cause the case to be in every way expedited. An appeal from the final judgment of such court will lie to the Supreme Court.

In the event the Attorney General fails to file such a request in any such proceeding, it shall be the duty of the chief judge of the district (or in his absence, the acting chief judge) in which the case is pending immediately to designate a judge in such district to hear and determine the case. In the event that no judge in the district is available to hear and determine the case, the chief judge of the district, or the acting chief judge, as the case may be, shall certify this fact to the chief judge of the circuit (or in his absence, the acting chief judge) who shall then designate a district or circuit judge of the circuit to hear and determine the case.

It shall be the duty of the judge designated pursuant to this section to assign the case for hearing at the earliest practicable date and to cause the case to be in every way expedited.

SEC. 207. (a) The district courts of the United States shall have jurisdiction of proceedings instituted pursuant to this title and shall exercise the same without regard to whether the aggrieved party shall have exhausted any administrative or other remedies that may be provided by law.

(b) The remedies provided in this title shall be the exclusive means of enforcing the rights based on this title, but nothing in this title shall preclude any individual or any State or local agency from asserting any right based on any other Federal or State law not inconsistent with this title, including any statute or ordinance requiring nondiscrimination in public establishments or accommodations, or from pursuing any remedy, civil or criminal, which may be available for the vindication or enforcement of such right.

Title III – Desegregation of Public Facilities

SEC. 301. (a) Whenever the Attorney General receives a complaint in writing signed by an individual to the effect that he is being deprived of or threatened with the loss of his right to the equal protection of the laws, on account of his race, color, religion, or national origin, by being denied equal utilization of any public facility which is owned, operated, or managed by or on behalf of any State or subdivision thereof, other than a public school or public college as defined in section 401 of title IV hereof, and the Attorney General believes the complaint is meritorious and certifies that the signer or signers of such complaint are unable, in his judgment, to initiate and maintain appropriate legal proceedings for relief and that the institution of an action will materially further the orderly progress of desegregation in public facilities, the Attorney General is authorized to institute for or in the name of the United States a civil action in any appropriate district court of the United States against such parties and for such relief as may be appropriate, and such court shall have and shall exercise jurisdiction of proceedings instituted pursuant to this section. The Attorney General may implead as defendants such additional parties as are or become necessary to the grant of effective relief hereunder.

(b) The Attorney General may deem a person or persons unable to initiate and maintain appropriate legal proceedings within the meaning of subsection

(a) of this section when such person or persons are unable, either directly or through other interested persons or organizations, to bear the expense of the litigation or to obtain effective legal representation; or whenever he is satisfied that the institution of such litigation would jeopardize the personal safety, employment, or economic standing of such person or persons, their families, or their property.

SEC.302. In any action or proceeding under this title the United States shall be liable for costs, including a reasonable attorney's fee, the same as a private person.

SEC. 303. Nothing in this title shall affect adversely the right of any person to sue for or obtain relief in any court against discrimination in any facility covered by this title.

SEC. 304. A complaint as used in this title is a writing or document within the meaning of section 1001, title 18, United States Code.

TITLE IV – DESEGREGATION OF PUBLIC EDUCATION

Definitions

SEC. 401. As used in this title –
(a) "Commissioner" means the Commissioner of Education.
(b) "Desegregation" means the assignment of students to public schools and within such schools without regard to their race, color, religion, or national origin, but "desegregation" shall not mean the assignment of students to public schools in order to overcome racial imbalance.
(c) "Public school" means any elementary or secondary educational institution, and "public college" means any institution of higher education or any technical or vocational school above the secondary school level, provided that such public school or public college is operated by a State, subdivision of a State, or governmental agency within a State, or operated wholly or predominantly from or through the use of governmental funds or property, or funds or property derived from a governmental source.
(d) "School board" means any agency or agencies which administer a system of one or more public schools and any other agency which is responsible for the assignment of students to or within such system.

SURVEY AND REPORT OF EDUCATIONAL OPPORTUNITIES

SEC. 402. The Commissioner shall conduct a survey and make a report to the President and the Congress, within two years of the enactment of this title, concerning the lack of availability of equal educational opportunities for individuals by reason of race, color, religion, or national origin in public educational institutions at all levels in the United States, its territories and possessions, and the District of Columbia.

TECHNICAL ASSISTANCE

SEC. 403. The Commissioner is authorized, upon the application of any school board, State, municipality, school district, or other governmental unit legally responsible for operating a public school or schools, to render technical assistance to such applicant in the preparation, adoption, and implementation of plans for the desegregation of public schools. Such technical assistance may, among other activities, include making available to such agencies information regarding effective methods of coping with special educational problems occasioned by desegregation, and making available to such agencies personnel of the Office of Education or other persons specially equipped to advise and assist them in coping with such problems.

TRAINING INSTITUTES

SEC. 404. The Commissioner is authorized to arrange, through grants or contracts, with institutions of higher education for the operation of short-term or regular session institutes for special training designed to improve the ability of teachers, supervisors, counselors, and other elementary or secondary school personnel to deal effectively with special educational problems occasioned by desegregation. Individuals who attend such an institute on a full-time basis may be paid stipends for the period of their attendance at such institute in amounts specified by the Commissioner in regulations, including allowances for travel to attend such institute.

Grants

SEC. 405. (a) The Commissioner is authorized, upon application of a school board, to make grants to such board to pay, in whole or in part, the cost of –

(1) giving to teachers and other school personnel inservice training in dealing with problems incident to desegregation, and

(2) employing specialists to advise in problems incident to desegregation.

(b) In determining whether to make a grant, and in fixing the amount thereof and the terms and conditions on which it will be made, the Commissioner shall take into consideration the amount available for grants under this section and the other applications which are pending before him; the financial condition of the applicant and the other resources available to it; the nature, extent, and gravity of its problems incident to desegregation; and such other factors as he finds relevant.

Payments

SEC. 406. Payments pursuant to a grant or contract under this title may be made (after necessary adjustments on account of previously made overpayments or underpayments) in advance or by way of reimbursement, and in such installments, as the Commissioner may determine.

Suits by the Attorney General

SEC. 407. (a) Whenever the Attorney General receives a complaint in writing –

(1) signed by a parent or group of parents to the effect that his or their minor children, as members of a class of persons similarly situated, are being deprived by a school board of the equal protection of the laws, or

(2) signed by an individual, or his parent, to the effect that he has been denied admission to or not permitted to continue in attendance at a public college by reason of race, color, religion, or national origin, and the Attorney General believes the complaint is meritorious and certifies that the signer or signers of such complaint are unable, in his judgment, to initiate and maintain appropriate legal proceedings for relief and that the institution of an action will materially further the orderly achievement of desegregation in public education, the Attorney General is authorized, after giving notice of such complaint to the appropriate school board or college authority and after certifying that he is satisfied that such board or authority has had a reasonable time to adjust the conditions alleged in such complaint, to institute for or in the name of the United States a civil action in any appropriate district court of the United States against such parties and for such relief as may be appropriate, and such court shall have and shall exercise jurisdiction of proceedings instituted pursuant to this section, provided that nothing herein shall empower any official or court of the United States to issue any order seeking to achieve a racial balance in any school by requiring the transportation of pupils or students from one school to another or one school district to another in order to achieve such racial balance, or otherwise enlarge the existing power of the court to insure compliance with constitutional standards. The Attorney General may implead as defendants such additional parties as are or become necessary to the grant of effective relief hereunder.

(b) The Attorney General may deem a person or persons unable to initiate and maintain appropriate legal proceedings within the meaning of subsection

(a) of this section when such person or persons are unable, either directly or through other interested persons or organizations, to bear the expense of the litigation or to obtain effective legal representation; or whenever he is satisfied that the institution of such litigation would jeopardize the personal safety, employment, or economic standing of such person or persons, their families, or their property.

(c) The term "parent" as used in this section includes any person standing in loco parentis. A "complaint" as used in this section is a writing or document within the meaning of section 1001, title 18, United States Code.

SEC. 408. In any action or proceeding under this title the United States shall be liable for costs the same as a private person.

SEC. 409. Nothing in this title shall affect adversely the right of any person to sue for or obtain relief in any court against discrimination in public education.

SEC. 410. Nothing in this title shall prohibit classification and assignment for reasons other than race, color, religion, or national origin.

Title V – Commission on Civil Rights

SEC. 501. Section 102 of the Civil Rights Act of 1957 (42 U.S.C. 1975a; 71 Stat. 634) is amended to read as follows:

"Rules of Procedure of the Commission Hearings

"SEC. 102. (a) At least thirty days prior to the commencement of any hearing, the Commission shall cause to be published in the Federal Register notice of the date on which such hearing is to commence, the place at which it is to be held and the subject of the hearing. The Chairman, or one designated by him to act as Chairman at a hearing of the Commission, shall announce in an opening statement the subject of the hearing.

"(b) A copy of the Commission's rules shall be made available to any witness before the Commission, and a witness compelled to appear before the Commission or required to produce written or other matter shall be served with a copy of the Commission's rules at the time of service of the subpoena.

"(c) Any person compelled to appear in person before the Commission shall be accorded the right to be accompanied and advised by counsel, who shall have the right to subject his client to reasonable examination, and to make objections on the record and to argue briefly the basis for such objections. The Commission shall proceed with reasonable dispatch to conclude any hearing in which it is engaged. Due regard shall be had for the convenience and necessity of witnesses.

"(d) The Chairman or Acting Chairman may punish breaches of order and decorum by censure and exclusion from the hearings.

"(e) If the Commission determines that evidence or testimony at any hearing may tend to defame, degrade, or incriminate any person, it shall receive such evidence or testimony or summary of such evidence or testimony in executive session. The Commission shall afford any person defamed, degraded, or incriminated by such evidence or testimony an opportunity to appear and be heard in executive session, with a reasonable number of additional witnesses requested by him, before deciding to use such evidence or testimony. In the event the Commission determines to release or use such evidence or testimony in such manner as to reveal publicly the identity of the person defamed, degraded, or incriminated, such evidence or testimony, prior to such public release or use, shall be given at a public session, and the Commission shall afford such person an opportunity to appear as a voluntary witness or to file a sworn statement in his behalf and to submit brief and pertinent sworn statements of others. The Commission shall receive and dispose of requests from such person to subpoena additional witnesses.

"(f) Except as provided in sections 102 and 105 (f) of this Act, the Chairman shall receive and the Commission shall dispose of requests to subpoena additional witnesses.

"(g) No evidence or testimony or summary of evidence or testimony taken in executive session may be released or used in public sessions without the consent of the Commission. Whoever releases or uses in public without the consent of the Commission such evidence or testimony taken in executive session shall be fined not more than $1,000, or imprisoned for not more than one year.

"(h) In the discretion of the Commission, witnesses may submit brief and pertinent sworn statements in writing for inclusion in the record. The Commission shall determine the pertinency of testimony and evidence adduced at its hearings.

"(i) Every person who submits data or evidence shall be entitled to retain or, on payment of lawfully prescribed costs, procure a copy or transcript thereof, except that a witness in a hearing held in executive session may for good cause be limited to inspection of the official transcript of his testimony. Transcript copies of public sessions may be obtained by the public upon the payment of the cost thereof. An accurate transcript shall be made of the testimony of all witnesses at all hearings, either public or executive sessions, of the Commission or of any subcommittee thereof.

"(j) A witness attending any session of the Commission shall receive $6 for each day's attendance and for the time necessarily occupied in going to and returning from the same, and 10 cents per mile for going from and returning to his place of residence. Witnesses who attend at points so far removed from their respective residences as to prohibit return thereto from day to day shall be entitled to an additional allowance of $10 per day for expenses of subsistence including the time necessarily occupied in going to and returning from the place of attendance. Mileage payments shall be tendered to the witness upon service of a subpoena issued on behalf of the Commission or any subcommittee thereof.

"(k) The Commission shall not issue any subpoena for the attendance and testimony of witnesses or for the production of written or other matter which would require the presence of the party subpoenaed at a hearing to be held outside of the State wherein the witness is found or resides or is domiciled or transacts business, or has appointed an agent for receipt of service of process except that, in any event, the Commission may issue subpoenas for the attendance and testimony of witnesses and the production of written or other matter at a hearing held within fifty miles of the place where the witness is found or resides or is domiciled or transacts business or has appointed an agent for receipt of service of process.

"(l) The Commission shall separately state and currently publish in the Federal Register (1) descriptions of its central and field organization including the established places at which, and methods whereby, the public may secure information or make requests; (2) statements of the general course and method by which its functions are channeled and determined, and (3) rules adopted as authorized by law. No person shall in any manner be subject to or required to resort to rules, organization, or procedure not so published."

SEC. 502. Section 103(a) of the Civil Rights Act of 1957 (42 U.S.C. 1975b(a); 71 Stat. 634) is amended to read as follows:

"SEC. 103. (a) Each member of the Commission who is not otherwise in the service of the Government of the United States shall receive the sum of $75 per day for each day spent in the work of the Commission, shall be paid actual travel expenses, and per diem in lieu of subsistence expenses when away from his usual place of residence, in accordance with section 5 of the Administrative Expenses Act of 1946, as amended (5 U.S.C 73b-2; 60 Stat. 808)."

SEC. 503. Section 103(b) of the Civil Rights Act of 1957 (42 U.S.C. 1975(b); 71 Stat. 634) is amended to read as follows:

"(b) Each member of the Commission who is otherwise in the service of the Government of the United States shall serve without compensation in addition to that received for such other service, but while engaged in the work of the Commission shall be paid actual travel expenses, and per diem in lieu of subsistence expenses when away from his usual place of residence, in accordance with the provisions of the Travel Expenses Act of 1949, as amended (5 U.S.C. 835 – 42; 63 Stat. 166)."

SEC. 504. (a) Section 104(a) of the Civil Rights Act of 1957 (42 U.S.C. 1975c(a); 71 Stat. 635), as amended, is further amended to read as follows:

"Duties of the Commission

"SEC. 104. (a) The Commission shall –

"(1) investigate allegations in writing under oath or affirmation that certain citizens of the United States are being deprived of their right to vote and have that vote counted by reason of their color, race, religion, or national origin; which writing, under oath or affirmation, shall set forth the facts upon which such belief or beliefs are based;

"(2) study and collect information concerning legal developments constituting a denial of equal protection of the laws under the Constitution because of race, color, religion or national origin or in the administration of justice;

"(3) appraise the laws and policies of the Federal Government with respect to denials of equal protection of the laws under the Constitution because of race, color, religion or national origin or in the administration of justice;

"(4) serve as a national clearinghouse for information in respect to denials of equal protection of the laws because of race, color, religion or national origin, including but not limited to the fields of voting, education, housing, employment, the use of public facilities, and transportation, or in the administration of justice;

"(5) investigate allegations, made in writing and under oath or affirmation, that citizens of the United States are unlawfully being accorded or denied the right to vote, or to have their votes properly counted, in any election of presidential electors, Members of the United States Senate, or of the House of Representatives, as a result of any patterns or practice of fraud or discrimination in the conduct of such election; and

"(6) Nothing in this or any other Act shall be construed as authorizing the Commission, its Advisory Committees, or any person under its supervision or control to inquire into or investigate any membership practices or internal operations of any fraternal organization, any college or university fraternity or sorority, any private club or any religious organization."

(b) Section 104(b) of the Civil Rights Act of 1957 (42 U.S.C. 1975c(b); 71 Stat. 635), as amended, is further amended by striking out the present subsection "(b)" and by substituting therefor:

"(b) The Commission shall submit interim reports to the President and to the Congress at such times as the Commission, the Congress or the President shall deem desirable, and shall submit to the President and to the Congress a final report of its activities, findings, and recommendations not later than January 31, 1968."

SEC. 505. Section 105(a) of the Civil Rights Act of 1957 (42 U.S.C. 1975d(a); 71 Stat. 636) is amended by striking out in the last sentence thereof "$50 per diem" and inserting in lieu thereof "$75 per diem."

SEC. 506. Section 105(f) and section 105(g) of the Civil Rights Act of 1957 (42 U.S.C. 1975d (f) and (g); 71 Stat. 636) are amended to read as follows:

"(f) The Commission, or on the authorization of the Commission any subcommittee of two or more members, at least one of whom shall be of each major political party, may, for the purpose of carrying out the provisions of this Act, hold such hearings and act at such times and places as the Commission or such authorized subcommittee may deem advisable. Subpoenas for the attendance and testimony of witnesses or the production of written or other matter may be issued in accordance with the rules of the Commission as contained in section 102 (j) and (k) of this Act, over the signature of the Chairman of the Commission or of such subcommittee, and may be served by any person designated by such Chairman. The holding of hearings by the Commission, or the appointment of a subcommittee to hold hearings pursuant to this subparagraph, must be approved by a majority of the Commission, or by a majority of the members present at a meeting at which at least a quorum of four members is present.

"(g) In case of contumacy or refusal to obey a subpoena, any district court of the United States or the United States court of any territory or possession, or the District Court of the United States for the District of Columbia, within the jurisdiction of which the inquiry is carried on or within the jurisdiction of which said person guilty of contumacy or refusal to obey is found or resides or is domiciled or transacts business, or has appointed an agent for receipt of service of process, upon application by the Attorney General of the United States shall have jurisdiction to issue to such person an order requiring such person to appear before the Commission or a subcommittee thereof, there to produce pertinent, relevant and non-privileged evidence if so ordered, or there to give testimony touching the matter under investigation; and any failure to obey such order of the court may be punished by said court as a contempt thereof."

SEC. 507. Section 105 of the Civil Rights Act of 1957 (42 U.S.C. 1975d; 71 Stat. 636), as amended by section 401 of the Civil Rights Act of 1960 (42 U.S.C. 1975d(h); 74 Stat. 89), is further amended by adding a new subsection at the end to read as follows:

"(i) The Commission shall have the power to make such rules and regulations as are necessary to carry out the purposes of this Act."

TITLE VI – NONDISCRIMINATION IN FEDERALLY ASSISTED PROGRAMS

SEC. 601. No person in the United States shall, on the ground of race, color, or national origin, be excluded from participation in, be denied the benefits of, or be subjected to discrimination under any program or activity receiving Federal financial assistance.

SEC. 602. Each Federal department and agency which is empowered to extend Federal financial assistance to any program or activity, by way of grant, loan, or contract other than a contract of insurance or guaranty, is authorized and directed to effectuate the provisions of section 601 with respect to such program or activity by issuing rules, regulations, or orders of general applicability which shall be consistent with achievement of the objectives of the statute authorizing the financial assistance in connection with which the action is taken. No such rule, regulation, or order shall become effective unless and until approved by the President. Compliance with any requirement adopted pursuant to this section may be effected (1) by the termination of or refusal to grant or to continue assistance under such program or activity to any recipient as to whom there has been an express finding on the record, after opportunity for hearing, of a failure to comply with such requirement, but such termination or refusal shall be limited to the particular political entity, or part thereof, or other recipient as to whom such a finding has been made and, shall be limited in its effect to the particular program, or part thereof, in which such non-compliance has been so found, or (2) by any other means authorized by law: Provided, however, That no such action shall be taken until the department or agency concerned has advised the appropriate person or persons of the failure to comply with the requirement and has determined that compliance cannot be secured by voluntary means. In the case of any action terminating, or refusing to grant or continue, assistance because of failure to comply with a requirement imposed pursuant to this section, the head of the federal department or agency shall file with the committees of the House and Senate having legislative jurisdiction over the program or activity involved a full written report of the circumstances and the grounds for such action. No such action shall become effective until thirty days have elapsed after the filing of such report.

SEC. 603. Any department or agency action taken pursuant to section 602 shall be subject to such judicial review as may otherwise be provided by law for similar action taken by such department or agency on other grounds. In the case of action, not otherwise subject to judicial review, terminating or refusing to grant or to continue financial assistance upon a finding of failure to comply with any requirement imposed pursuant to section 602, any person aggrieved (including any State or political subdivision thereof and any agency of either) may obtain judicial review of such action in accordance with section 10 of the Administrative Procedure Act, and such action shall not be deemed committed to unreviewable agency discretion within the meaning of that section.

SEC. 604. Nothing contained in this title shall be construed to authorize action under this title by any department or agency with respect to any employment practice of any employer, employment agency, or labor organization except where a primary objective of the Federal financial assistance is to provide employment.

SEC. 605. Nothing in this title shall add to or detract from any existing authority with respect to any program or activity under which Federal financial assistance is extended by way of a contract of insurance or guaranty.

Title VII – Equal Employment Opportunity

Definitions

SEC. 701. For the purposes of this title –

(a) The term "person" includes one or more individuals, labor unions, partnerships, associations, corporations, legal representatives, mutual companies, joint-stock companies, trusts, unincorporated organizations, trustees, trustees in bankruptcy, or receivers.

(b) The term "employer" means a person engaged in an industry affecting commerce who has twenty-five or more employees for each working day in each of twenty or more calendar weeks in the current or preceding calendar year, and any agent of such a person, but such term does not include (1) the United States, a corporation wholly owned by the Government of the United States, an Indian tribe, or a State or political subdivision thereof, (2) a bona fide private membership club (other than a labor organization) which is exempt from taxation under section 501(c) of the Internal Revenue Code of 1954: Provided, That during the first year after the effective date prescribed in subsection (a) of section 716, persons having fewer than one hundred employees (and their agents) shall not be considered employers, and, during the second year after such date, persons having fewer than seventy-five employees (and their agents) shall not be considered employers, and, during the third year after such date, persons having fewer than fifty employees (and their agents) shall not be considered employers: Provided further, That it shall be the policy of the United States to insure equal employment opportunities for Federal employees without discrimination because of race, color, religion, sex or national origin and the President shall utilize his existing authority to effectuate this policy.

(c) The term "employment agency" means any person regularly undertaking with or without compensation to procure employees for an employer or to procure for employees opportunities to work for an employer and includes an agent of such a person; but shall not include an agency of the United States, or an agency of a State or political subdivision of a State, except that such term shall include the United States Employment Service and the system of State and local employment services receiving Federal assistance.

(d) The term "labor organization" means a labor organization engaged in an industry affecting commerce, and any agent of such an organization, and includes any organization of any kind, any agency, or employee representation committee, group, association, or plan so engaged in which employees participate and which exists for the purpose, in whole or in part, of dealing with employers concerning grievances, labor disputes, wages, rates of pay, hours, or other terms or conditions of employment, and any conference, general committee, joint or system board, or joint council so engaged which is subordinate to a national or international labor organization.

(e) A labor organization shall be deemed to be engaged in an industry affecting commerce if (1) it maintains or operates a hiring hall or hiring office which procures employees for an employer or procures for employees opportunities to work for an employer, or (2) the number of its members (or, where it is a labor organization composed of other labor organizations or their representatives, if the aggregate number of the members of such other labor organization) is (A) one hundred or more during the first year after the effective date prescribed in subsection (a) of section 716, (B) seventy-five or more during the second year after such date or fifty or more during the third year, or (C) twenty-five or more thereafter, and such labor organization –

(1) is the certified representative of employees under the provisions of the National Labor Relations Act, as amended, or the Railway Labor Act, as amended;

(2) although not certified, is a national or international labor organization or a local labor organization recognized or acting as the representative of employees of an employer or employers engaged in an industry affecting commerce; or

(3) has chartered a local labor organization or subsidiary body which is representing or actively seeking to represent employees of employers within the meaning of paragraph (1) or (2); or

(4) has been chartered by a labor organization representing or actively seeking to represent employees within the meaning of paragraph (1) or (2) as the local or subordinate body through which such employees may enjoy membership or become affiliated with such labor organization; or

(5) is a conference, general committee, joint or system board, or joint council subordinate to a national or international labor organization, which includes a labor organization engaged in an industry affecting commerce within the meaning of any of the preceding paragraphs of this subsection.

(f) The term "employee" means an individual employed by an employer.

(g) The term "commerce" means trade, traffic, commerce, transportation, transmission, or communication among the several States; or between a State and any place outside thereof; or within the District of Columbia, or a possession of the United States; or between points in the same State but through a point outside thereof.

(h) The term "industry affecting commerce" means any activity, business, or industry in commerce or in which a labor dispute would hinder or obstruct commerce or the free flow of commerce and includes any activity or industry "affecting commerce" within the meaning of the Labor-Management Reporting and Disclosure Act of 1959.

(i) The term "State" includes a State of the United States, the District of Columbia, Puerto Rico, the Virgin Islands, American Samoa, Guam, Wake Island, The Canal Zone, and Outer Continental Shelf Lands defined in the Outer Continental Shelf Lands Act.

Exemption

SEC. 702. This title shall not apply to an employer with respect to the employment of aliens outside any State, or to a religious corporation, association, or society with respect to the employment of individuals of a particular religion to perform work connected with the carrying on by such corporation, association, or society of its religious activities or to an educational institution with respect to the employment of individuals to perform work connected with the educational activities of such institution.

Discrimination Because of Race, Color, Religion, Sex, or National Origin

SEC. 703. (a) It shall be an unlawful employment practice for an employer –

(1) to fail or refuse to hire or to discharge any individual, or otherwise to discriminate against any individual with respect to his compensation, terms, conditions, or privileges of employment, because of such individual's race, color, religion, sex, or national origin; or

(2) to limit, segregate, or classify his employees in any way which would deprive or tend to deprive any individual of employment opportunities or otherwise adversely affect his status as an employee, because of such individual's race, color, religion, sex, or national origin.

(b) It shall be an unlawful employment practice for an employment agency to fail or refuse to refer for employment, or otherwise to discriminate against, any individual because of his race, color, religion, sex, or national origin, or to classify or refer for employment any individual on the basis of his race, color, religion, sex, or national origin.

(c) It shall be an unlawful employment practice for a labor organization –

(1) to exclude or to expel from its membership, or otherwise to discriminate against, any individual because of his race, color, religion, sex, or national origin;

(2) to limit, segregate, or classify its membership, or to classify or fail or refuse to refer for employment any individual, in any way which would deprive or tend to deprive any individual of employment opportunities, or would limit such employment opportunities or otherwise adversely affect his status as an employee or as an applicant for employment, because of such individual's race, color, religion, sex, or national origin; or

(3) to cause or attempt to cause an employer to discriminate against an individual in violation of this section.

(d) It shall be an unlawful employment practice for any employer, labor organization, or joint labor-management committee controlling apprenticeship or other training or retraining, including on-the-job training programs to discriminate against any individual because of his race, color, religion, sex, or national origin in admission to, or employment in, any program established to provide apprenticeship or other training.

(c) Notwithstanding any other provision of this title, (1) it shall not be an unlawful employment practice for an employer to hire and employ employees, for an employment agency to classify, or refer for employment any individual, for a labor organization to classify its membership or to classify or refer for employment any individual, or for an employer, labor organization, or joint labor-management committee controlling apprenticeship or other training or retraining programs to admit or employ any individual in any such program, on the basis of his religion, sex, or national origin in those certain instances where religion, sex, or national origin is a bona fide occupational qualification reasonably necessary to the normal operation of that particular business or enterprise, and (2) it shall not be an unlawful employment practice for a school, college, university, or other educational institution or institution of learning to hire and employ employees of a particular religion if such school, college, university, or other educational institution or institution of learning is, in whole or in substantial part, owned, supported, controlled, or managed by a particular religion or by a particular religious corporation, association, or society, or if the curriculum of such school, college, university, or other educational institution or institution of learning is directed toward the propagation of a particular religion.

(f) As used in this title, the phrase "unlawful employment practice" shall not be deemed to include any action or measure taken by an employer, labor organization, joint labor-management committee, or employment agency with respect to an individual who is a member of the Communist Party of the United States or of any other organization required to register as a Communist-action or Communist-front organization by final order of the Subversive Activities Control Board pursuant to the Subversive Activities Control Act of 1950.

(g) Notwithstanding any other provision of this title, it shall not be an unlawful employment practice for an employer to fail or refuse to hire and employ any individual for any position, for an employer to discharge any individual from any position, or for an employment agency to fail or refuse to refer any individual for employment in any position, or for a labor organization to fail or refuse to refer any individual for employment in any position, if –

(1) the occupancy of such position, or access to the premises in or upon which any part of the duties of such position is performed or is to be performed, is subject to any requirement imposed in the interest of the national security of the United States under any security program in effect pursuant to or administered under any statute of the United States or any Executive order of the President; and

(2) such individual has not fulfilled or has ceased to fulfill that requirement.

(h) Notwithstanding any other provision of this title, it shall not be an unlawful employment practice for an employer to apply different standards of compensation, or different terms, conditions, or privileges of employment pursuant to a bona fide seniority or merit system, or a system which measures earnings by quantity or quality of production or to employees who work in different locations, provided that such differences are not the result of an intention to discriminate because of race, color, religion, sex, or national origin, nor shall it be an unlawful employment practice for an employer to give and to act upon the results of any professionally developed ability test provided that such test, its administration or action upon the results is not designed, intended or used to discriminate because of race, color, religion, sex or national origin. It shall not be an unlawful employment practice under this title for any employer to differentiate upon the basis of sex in determining the amount of the wages or compensation paid or to be paid to employees of such employer if such differentiation is authorized by the provisions of section 6(d) of the Fair Labor Standards Act of 1938, as amended (29 U.S.C. 206(d)).

(i) Nothing contained in this title shall apply to any business or enterprise on or near an Indian reservation with respect to any publicly announced employment practice of such business or enterprise under which a preferential treatment is given to any individual because he is an Indian living on or near a reservation.

(j) Nothing contained in this title shall be interpreted to require any employer, employment agency, labor organization, or joint labor-management committee subject to this title to grant preferential treatment to any individual or to any group because of the race, color, religion, sex, or national origin of such individual or group on account of an imbalance which may exist with respect to the total number or percentage of persons of any race, color, religion, sex, or national origin employed by any employer, referred or classified for employment by any employment agency or labor organization, admitted to membership or classified by any labor organization, or admitted to, or employed in, any apprenticeship or other training program, in comparison with the total number or percentage of persons of such race, color, religion, sex, or national origin in any community, State, section, or other area, or in the available work force in any community, State, section, or other area.

Other Unlawful Employment Practices

SEC. 704. (a) It shall be an unlawful employment practice for an employer to discriminate against any of his employees or applicants for employment, for an employment agency to discriminate against any individual, or for a labor organization to discriminate against any member thereof or applicant for membership, because he has opposed, any practice made an unlawful employment practice by this title, or because he has made a charge, testified, assisted, or participated in any manner in an investigation, proceeding, or hearing under this title.

(b) It shall be an unlawful employment practice for an employer, labor organization, or employment agency to print or publish or cause to be printed or published any notice or advertisement relating to employment by such an employer or membership in or any classification or referral for employment by such a labor organization, or relating to any classification or referral for employment by such an employment agency, indicating any preference, limitation, specification, or discrimination, based on race, color, religion, sex, or national origin, except that such a notice or advertisement may indicate a preference, limitation, specification, or discrimination based on religion, sex, or national origin when religion, sex, or national origin is a bona fide occupational qualification for employment.

Equal Employment Opportunity
Commission

SEC. 705. (a) There is hereby created a Commission to be known as the Equal Employment Opportunity Commission, which shall be composed of five members, not more than three of whom shall be members of the same political party, who shall be appointed by the President by and with the advice and consent of the Senate. One of the original members shall be appointed for a term of one year, one for a term of two years, one for a term of three years, one for a term of four years, and one for a term of five years, beginning from the date of enactment of this title, but their successors shall be appointed for terms of five years each, except that any individual chosen to fill a vacancy shall be appointed only for the unexpired term of the member whom he shall succeed. The President shall designate one member to serve as Chairman of the Commission, and one member to serve as Vice Chairman. The Chairman shall be responsible on behalf of the Commission for the administrative operations of the Commission, and shall appoint, in accordance with the civil service laws, such officers, agents, attorneys, and employees as it deems necessary to assist it in the performance of its functions and to fix their compensation in accordance with the Classification Act of 1949, as amended. The Vice Chairman shall act as Chairman in the absence or disability of the Chairman or in the event of a vacancy in that office.

(b) A vacancy in the Commission shall not impair the right of the remaining members to exercise all the powers of the Commission and three members thereof shall constitute a quorum.

(c) The Commission shall have an official seal which shall be judicially noticed.

(d) The Commission shall at the close of each fiscal year report to the Congress and to the President concerning the action it has taken; the names, salaries, and duties of all individuals in its employ and the moneys it has disbursed; and shall make such further reports on the cause of and means of eliminating discrimination and such recommendations for further legislation as may appear desirable.

(e) The Federal Executive Pay Act of 1956, as amended (5 U.S.C. 2201-2209), is further amended ––

(1) by adding to section 105 thereof (5 U.S.C. 2204) the following clause:

"(32) Chairman, Equal Employment Opportunity Commission"; and

(2) by adding to clause (45) of section 106(a) thereof (5 U.S.C. 2205(a)) the following: "Equal Employment Opportunity Commission (4)."

(f) The principal office of the Commission shall be in or near the District of Columbia, but it may meet or exercise any or all its powers at any other place. The Commission may establish such regional or State offices as it deems necessary to accomplish the purpose of this title.

(g) The Commission shall have power --

(1) to cooperate with and, with their consent, utilize regional, State, local, and other agencies, both public and private, and individuals;

(2) to pay to witnesses whose depositions are taken or who are summoned before the Commission or any of its agents the same witness and mileage fees as are paid to witnesses in the courts of the United States;

(3) to furnish to persons subject to this title such technical assistance as they may request to further their compliance with this title or an order issued thereunder;

(4) upon the request of (i) any employer, whose employees or some of them, or (ii) any labor organization, whose members or some of them, refuse or threaten to refuse to cooperate in effectuating the provisions of this title, to assist in such effectuation by conciliation or such other remedial action as is provided by this title;

(5) to make such technical studies as are appropriate to effectuate the purposes and policies of this title and to make the results of such studies available to the public;

(6) to refer matters to the Attorney General with recommendations for intervention in a civil action brought by an aggrieved party under section 706, or for the institution of a civil action by the Attorney General under section 707, and to advise, consult, and assist the Attorney General on such matters.

(h) Attorneys appointed under this section may, at the direction of the Commission, appear for and represent the Commission in any case in court.

(i) The Commission shall, in any of its educational or promotional activities, cooperate with other departments and agencies in the performance of such educational and promotional activities.

(j) All officers, agents, attorneys, and employees of the Commission shall be subject to the provisions of section 9 of the Act of August 2, 1939, as amended (the Hatch Act), notwithstanding any exemption contained in such section.

*Prevention of Unlawful
Employment Practices*

SEC. 706. (a) Whenever it is charged in writing under oath by a person claiming to be aggrieved, or a written charge has been filed by a member of the Commission where he has reasonable cause to believe a violation of this title has occurred (and such charge sets forth the facts upon which it is based) that an employer, employment agency, or labor organization has engaged in an unlawful employment practice, the Commission shall furnish such employer, employment agency, or labor organization (hereinafter referred to as the "respondent") with a copy of such charge and shall make an investigation of such charge, provided that such charge shall not be made public by the Commission. If the Commission shall determine, after such investigation, that there is reasonable cause to believe that the charge is true, the Commission shall endeavor to eliminate any such alleged unlawful employment practice by informal methods of conference, conciliation, and persuasion. Nothing said or done during and as a part of such endeavors may be made public by the Commission without the written consent of the parties, or used as evidence in a subsequent proceeding. Any officer or employee of the Commission, who shall make public in any manner whatever any information in violation of this subsection shall be deemed guilty of a misdemeanor and upon conviction thereof shall be fined not more than $1,000 or imprisoned not more than one year.

(b) In the case of an alleged unlawful employment practice occurring in a State, or political subdivision of a State, which has a State or local law prohibiting the unlawful employment practice alleged and establishing or authorizing a State or local authority to grant or seek relief from such practice or to institute criminal proceedings with respect thereto upon receiving notice thereof, no charge may be filed under subsection (a) by the person aggrieved before the expiration of sixty days after proceedings have been commenced under the State or local law, unless such proceedings have been earlier terminated, provided that such sixty-day period shall be extended to one hundred and twenty days during the first year after the effective date of such State or local law. If any requirement for the commencement of such proceedings is imposed by a State or local authority other than a requirement of the filing of a written and signed statement of the facts upon which the proceeding is based, the proceeding shall be deemed to have been commenced for the purposes of this subsection at the time such statement is sent by registered mail to the appropriate State or local authority.

(c) In the case of any charge filed by a member of the Commission alleging an unlawful employment practice occurring in a State or political subdivision of a State, which has a State or local law prohibiting the practice alleged and establishing or authorizing a State or local authority to grant or seek relief from such practice or to institute criminal proceedings with respect thereto upon receiving notice thereof, the Commission shall, before taking any action with respect to such charge, notify the appropriate State or local officials and, upon request, afford them a reasonable time, but not less than sixty days (provided that such sixty-day period shall be extended to one hundred and twenty days during the first year after the effective day of such State or local law), unless a shorter period is requested, to act under such State or local law to remedy the practice alleged.

(d) A charge under subsection (a) shall be filed within ninety days after the alleged unlawful employment practice occurred, except that in the case of an unlawful employment practice with respect to which the person aggrieved has followed the procedure set out in subsection (b), such charge shall be filed by the person aggrieved within two hundred and ten days after the alleged unlawful employment practice occurred, or within thirty days after receiving notice that the State or local agency has terminated the proceedings under the State or local law, whichever is earlier, and a copy of such charge shall be filed by the Commission with the State or local agency.

(e) If within thirty days after a charge is filed with the Commission or within thirty days after expiration of any period of reference under subsection (c) (except that in either case such period may be extended to not more than sixty days upon a determination by the Commission that further efforts to secure voluntary compliance are warranted), the Commission has been unable to obtain voluntary compliance with this title, the Commission shall so notify the person aggrieved and a civil action may, within thirty days thereafter, be brought against the respondent named in the charge (1) by the person claiming to be aggrieved, or (2) if such charge was filed by a member of the Commission, by any person whom the charge alleges was aggrieved by the alleged unlawful employment practice. Upon application by the complainant and in such circumstances as the court may deem just, the court may appoint an attorney for such complainant and may authorize the commencement of the action without the payment of fees, costs, or security. Upon timely application, the court may, in its discretion, permit the Attorney General to intervene in such civil action if he certifies that the case is of general public importance. Upon request, the court may, in its discretion, stay further proceedings for not more than sixty days pending the termination of State or local proceedings described in subsection (b) or the efforts of the Commission to obtain voluntary compliance.

(f) Each United States district court and each United States court of a place subject to the jurisdiction of the United States shall have jurisdiction of actions brought under this title. Such an action may be brought in any judicial district in the State in which the unlawful employment practice is alleged to have been committed, in the judicial district in which the employment records relevant to such practice are maintained and administered, or in the judicial district in which the plaintiff would have worked but for the alleged unlawful employment practice, but if the respondent is not found within any such district, such an action may be brought within the judicial district in which the respondent has his principal office. For purposes of sections 1404 and 1406 of title 28 of the United States Code, the judicial district in which the respondent has his principal office shall in all cases be considered a district in which the action might have been brought.

(g) If the court finds that the respondent has intentionally engaged in or is intentionally engaging in an unlawful employment practice charged in the complaint, the court may enjoin the respondent from engaging in such unlawful employment practice, and order such affirmative action as may be appropriate, which may include reinstatement or hiring of employees, with or without back pay (payable by the employer, employment agency, or labor organization, as the case may be, responsible for the unlawful employment practice). Interim earnings or amounts earnable with reasonable diligence by the person or persons discriminated against shall operate to reduce the back pay otherwise allowable. No order of the court shall require the admission or reinstatement of an individual as a member of a union or the hiring, reinstatement, or promotion of an individual as an employee, or the payment to him of any back pay, if such individual was refused admission, suspended, or expelled or was refused employment or advancement or was suspended or discharged for any reason other than discrimination on account of race, color, religion, sex or national origin or in violation of section 704(a).

(h) The provisions of the Act entitled "An Act to amend the Judicial Code and to define and limit the jurisdiction of courts sitting in equity, and for other purposes," approved March 23, 1932 (29 U.S.C. 101-115), shall not apply with respect to civil actions brought under this section.

(i) In any case in which an employer, employment agency, or labor organization fails to comply with an order of a court issued in a civil action brought under subsection (e), the Commission may commence proceedings to compel compliance with such order.

(j) Any civil action brought under subsection (e) and any proceedings brought under subsection (i) shall be subject to appeal as provided in sections 1291 and 1292, title 28, United States Code.

(k) In any action or proceeding under this title the court, in its discretion, may allow the prevailing party, other than the Commission or the United States, a reasonable attorney's fee as part of the costs, and the Commission and the United States shall be liable for costs the same as a private person.

SEC. 707. (a) Whenever the Attorney General has reasonable cause to believe that any person or group of persons is engaged in a pattern or practice of resistance to the full enjoyment of any of the rights secured by this title, and that the pattern or practice is of such a nature and is intended to deny the full exercise of the rights herein described, the Attorney General may bring a civil action in the appropriate district court of the United States by filing with it a complaint (1) signed by him (or in his absence the Acting Attorney General), (2) setting forth facts pertaining to such pattern or practice, and (3) requesting such relief, including an application for a permanent or temporary injunction, restraining order or other order against the person or persons responsible for such pattern or practice, as he deems necessary to insure the full enjoyment of the rights herein described.

(b) The district courts of the United States shall have and shall exercise jurisdiction of proceedings instituted pursuant to this section, and in any such proceeding the Attorney General may file with the clerk of such court a request that a court of three judges be convened to hear and determine the case. Such request by the Attorney General shall be accompanied by a certificate that, in his opinion, the case is of general public importance. A copy of the certificate and request for a three-judge court shall be immediately furnished by such clerk to the chief judge of the circuit (or in his absence, the presiding circuit judge of the circuit) in which the case is pending. Upon receipt of such request it shall be the duty of the chief judge of the circuit or the presiding circuit judge, as the case may be, to designate immediately three judges in such circuit, of whom at least one shall be a circuit judge and another of whom shall be a district judge of the court in which the proceeding was instituted, to hear and determine such case, and it shall be the duty of the judges so designated to assign the case for hearing at the earliest practicable date, to participate in the hearing and determination thereof and to cause the case to be in every way expedited. An appeal from the final judgment of such court will lie to the Supreme Court.

In the event the Attorney General fails to file such a request in any such proceeding, it shall be the duty of the chief judge of the district (or in his absence, the acting chief judge) in which the case is pending immediately to designate a judge in such district to hear and determine the case. In the event that no judge in the district is available to hear and determine the case, the chief judge of the district, or the acting chief judge, as the case may be, shall certify this fact to the chief judge of the circuit (or in his absence, the acting chief judge) who shall then designate a district or circuit judge of the circuit to hear and determine the case.

It shall be the duty of the judge designated pursuant to this section to assign the case for hearing at the earliest practicable date and to cause the case to be in every way expedited.

Effect on State Laws

SEC. 708. Nothing in this title shall be deemed to exempt or relieve any person from any liability, duty, penalty, or punishment provided by any present or future law of any State or political subdivision of a State, other than any such law which purports to require or permit the doing of any act which would be an unlawful employment practice under this title.

Investigation, Inspections, Records,
State Agencies

SEC. 709. (a) In connection with any investigation of a charge filed under section 706, the Commission or its designated representative shall at all reasonable times have access to, for the purposes of examination, and the right to copy any evidence of any person being investigated or proceeded against that relates to unlawful employment practices covered by this title and is relevant to the charge under investigation.

(b) The Commission may cooperate with State and local agencies charged with the administration of State fair employment practices laws and, with the consent of such agencies, may for the purpose of carrying out its functions and duties under this title and within the limitation of funds appropriated specifically for such purpose, utilize the services of such agencies and their employees and, notwithstanding any other provision of law, may reimburse such agencies and their employees for services rendered to assist the Commission in carrying out this title. In furtherance of such cooperative efforts, the Commission may enter into written agreements with such State or local agencies and such agreements may include provisions under which the Commission shall refrain from processing a charge in any cases or class of cases specified in such agreements and under which no person may bring a civil action under section 706 in any cases or class of cases so specified, or under which the Commission shall relieve any person or class of persons in such State or locality from requirements imposed under this section. The Commission shall rescind any such agreement whenever it determines that the agreement no longer serves the interest of effective enforcement of this title.

(c) Except as provided in subsection (d), every employer, employment agency, and labor organization subject to this title shall (1) make and keep such records relevant to the determinations of whether unlawful employment practices have been or are being committed, (2) preserve such records for such periods, and (3) make such reports therefrom, as the Commission shall prescribe by regulation or order, after public hearing, as reasonable, necessary, or appropriate for the enforcement of this title or the regulations or orders thereunder. The Commission shall, by regulation, require each employer, labor organization, and joint labor-management committee subject to this title which controls an apprenticeship or other training program to maintain such records as are reasonably necessary to carry out the purpose of this title, including, but not limited to, a list of applicants who wish to participate in such program, including the chronological order in which such applications were received, and shall furnish to the Commission, upon request, a detailed description of the manner in which persons are selected to participate in the apprenticeship or other training program. Any employer, employment agency, labor organization, or joint labor-management committee which believes that the application to it of any regulation or order issued under this section would result in undue hardship may (1) apply to the Commission for an exemption from the application of such regulation or order, or (2) bring a civil action in the United States district court for the district where such records are kept. If the Commission or the court, as the case may be, finds that the application of the regulation or order to the employer, employment agency, or labor organization in question would impose an undue hardship, the Commission or the court, as the case may be, may grant appropriate relief.

(d) The provisions of subsection (c) shall not apply to any employer, employment agency, labor organization, or joint labor-management committee with respect to matters occurring in any State or political subdivision thereof which has a fair employment practice law during any period in which such employer, employment agency, labor organization, or joint labor-management committee is subject to such law, except that the Commission may require such notations on records which such employer, employment agency, labor organization, or joint labor-management committee keeps or is required to keep as are necessary because of differences in coverage or methods of enforcement between the State or local law and the provisions of this title. Where an employer is required by Executive Order 10925, issued March 6, 1961, or by any other Executive order prescribing fair employment practices for Government contractors and subcontractors, or by rules or regulations issued thereunder, to file reports relating to his employment practices with any Federal agency or committee, and he is substantially in compliance with such requirements, the Commission shall not require him to file additional reports pursuant to subsection (c) of this section.

(e) It shall be unlawful for any officer or employee of the Commission to make public in any manner whatever any information obtained by the Commission pursuant to its authority under this section prior to the institution of any proceeding under this title involving such information. Any officer or employee of the Commission who shall make public in any manner whatever any information in violation of this subsection shall be guilty of a misdemeanor and, upon conviction thereof, shall be fined not more than $1,000, or imprisoned not more than one year.

Investigatory Powers

SEC. 710. (a) For the purposes of any investigation of a charge filed under the authority contained in section 706, the Commission shall have authority to examine witnesses under oath and to require the production of documentary evidence relevant or material to the charge under investigation.

(b) If the respondent named in a charge filed under section 706 fails or refuses to comply with a demand of the Commission for permission to examine or to copy evidence in conformity with the provisions of section 709(a), or if any person required to comply with the provisions of section 709 (c) or (d) fails or refuses to do so, or if any person fails or refuses to comply with a demand by the Commission to give testimony under oath, the United States district court for the district in which such person is found, resides, or transacts business, shall, upon application of the Commission, have jurisdiction to issue to such person an order requiring him to comply with the provisions of section 709 (c) or (d) or to comply with the demand of the Commission, but the attendance of a witness may not be required outside the State where he is found, resides, or transacts business and the production of evidence may not be required outside the State where such evidence is kept.

(c) Within twenty days after the service upon any person charged under section 706 of a demand by the Commission for the production of documentary evidence or for permission to examine or to copy evidence in conformity with the provisions of section 709(a), such person may file in the district court of the United States for the judicial district in which he resides, is found, or transacts business, and serve upon the Commission a petition for an order of such court modifying or setting aside such demand. The time allowed for compliance with the demand in whole or in part as deemed proper and ordered by the court shall not run during the pendency of such petition in the court. Such petition shall specify each ground upon which the petitioner relies in seeking such relief, and may be based upon any failure of such demand to comply with the provisions of this title or with the limitations generally applicable to compulsory process or upon any constitutional or other legal right or privilege of such person. No objection which is not raised by such a petition may be urged in the defense to a proceeding initiated by the Commission under subsection (b) for enforcement of such a demand unless such proceeding is commenced by the Commission prior to the expiration of the twenty-day period, or unless the court determines that the defendant could not reasonably have been aware of the availability of such ground of objection.

(d) In any proceeding brought by the Commission under subsection (b), except as provided in subsection (c) of this section, the defendant may petition the court for an order modifying or setting aside the demand of the Commission.

SEC. 711. (a) Every employer, employment agency, and labor organization, as the case may be, shall post and keep posted in conspicuous places upon its premises where notices to employees, applicants for employment, and members are customarily posted a notice to be prepared or approved by the Commission setting forth excerpts from, or summaries of, the pertinent provisions of this title and information pertinent to the filing of a complaint.

(b) A willful violation of this section shall be punishable by a fine of not more than $100 for each separate offense.

Veterans' Preference

SEC. 712. Nothing contained in this title shall be construed to repeal or modify any Federal, State, territorial, or local law creating special rights or preference for veterans.

Rules and Regulations

SEC. 713. (a) The Commission shall have authority from time to time to issue, amend, or rescind suitable procedural regulations to carry out the provisions of this title. Regulations issued under this section shall be in conformity with the standards and limitations of the Administrative Procedure Act.

(b) In any action or proceeding based on any alleged unlawful employment practice, no person shall be subject to any liability or punishment for or on account of (1) the commission by such person of an unlawful employment practice if he pleads and proves that the act or omission complained of was in good faith, in conformity with, and in reliance on any written interpretation or opinion of the Commission, or (2) the failure of such person to publish and file any information required by any provision of this title if he pleads and proves that he failed to publish and file such information in good faith, in conformity with the instructions of the Commission issued under this title regarding the filing of such information. Such a defense, if established, shall be a bar to the action or proceeding, notwithstanding that (A) after such act or omission, such interpretation or opinion is modified or rescinded or is determined by judicial authority to be invalid or of no legal effect, or (B) after publishing or filing the description and annual reports, such publication or filing is determined by judicial authority not to be in conformity with the requirements of this title.

Forcibly Resisting the Commission
or its Representatives

SEC. 714. The provisions of section 111, title 18, United States Code, shall apply to officers, agents, and employees of the Commission in the performance of their official duties.

Special Study by
Secretary of Labor

SEC. 715. The Secretary of Labor shall make a full and complete study of the factors which might tend to result in discrimination in employment because of age and of the consequences of such discrimination on the economy and individuals affected. The Secretary of Labor shall make a report to the Congress not later than June 30, 1965, containing the results of such study and shall include in such report such recommendations for legislation to prevent arbitrary discrimination in employment because of age as he determines advisable.

Effective Date

SEC. 716. (a) This title shall become effective one year after the date of its enactment.

(b) Notwithstanding subsection (a), sections of this title other than sections 703, 704, 706, and 707 shall become effective immediately.

(c) The President shall, as soon as feasible after the enactment of this title, convene one or more conferences for the purpose of enabling the leaders of groups whose members will be affected by this title to become familiar with the rights afforded and obligations imposed by its provisions, and for the purpose of making plans which will result in the fair and effective administration of this title when all of its provisions become effective. The President shall invite the participation in such conference or conferences of (1) the members of the President's Committee on Equal Employment Opportunity, (2) the members of the Commission on Civil Rights, (3) representatives of State and local agencies engaged in furthering equal employment opportunity, (4) representatives of private agencies engaged in furthering equal employment opportunity, and (5) representatives of employers, labor organizations, and employment agencies who will be subject to this title.

TITLE VIII—REGISTRATION AND VOTING STATISTICS

SEC. 801. The Secretary of Commerce shall promptly conduct a survey to compile registration and voting statistics in such geographic areas as may be recommended by the Commission on Civil Rights. Such a survey and compilation shall, to the extent recommended by the Commission on Civil Rights, only include a count of persons of voting age by race, color, and national origin, and determination of the extent to which such persons are registered to vote, and have voted in any statewide primary or general election in which the Members of the United States House of Representatives are nominated or elected, since January 1, 1960. Such information shall also be collected and compiled in connection with the Nineteenth Decennial Census, and at such other times as the Congress may prescribe. The provisions of section 9 and chapter 7 of title 13, United States Code, shall apply to any survey, collection, or compilation of registration and voting statistics carried out under this title: Provided, however, That no person shall be compelled to disclose his race, color, national origin, or questioned about his political party affiliation, how he voted, or the reasons therefore, nor shall any penalty be imposed for his failure or refusal to make such disclosure. Every person interrogated orally, by written survey or questionnaire or by any other means with respect to such information shall be fully advised with respect to his right to fail or refuse to furnish such information.

TITLE IX—INTERVENTION AND
PROCEDURE AFTER REMOVAL
IN CIVIL RIGHTS CASES

SEC. 901. Title 28 of the United States Code, section 1447(d), is amended to read as follows:
"An order remanding a case to the State court from which it was removed is not reviewable on appeal or otherwise, except that an order remanding a case to the State court from which it was removed pursuant to section 1443 of this title shall be reviewable by appeal or otherwise."
SEC. 902. Whenever an action has been commenced in any court of the United States seeking relief from the denial of equal protection of the laws under the fourteenth amendment to the Constitution on account of race, color, religion, or national origin, the Attorney General for or in the name of the United States may intervene in such action upon timely application if the

Attorney General certifies that the case is of general public importance. In such action the United States shall be entitled to the same relief as if it had instituted the action.

Title X—Establishment of
Community Relations Service

SEC. 1001. (a) There is hereby established in and as a part of the Department of Commerce a Community Relations Service (hereinafter referred to as the "Service"), which shall be headed by a Director who shall be appointed by the President with the advice and consent of the Senate for a term of four years. The Director is authorized to appoint, subject to the civil service laws and regulations, such other personnel as may be necessary to enable the Service to carry out its functions and duties, and to fix their compensation in accordance with the Classification Act of 1949, as amended. The Director is further authorized to procure services as authorized by section 15 of the Act of August 2, 1946 (60 Stat. 810; 5 U.S.C. 55(a)), but at rates for individuals not in excess of $75 per diem.

(b) Section 106(a) of the Federal Executive Pay Act of 1956, as amended (5 U.S.C. 2205(a)), is further amended by adding the following clause thereto:

"(52) Director, Community Relations Service."

SEC. 1002. It shall be the function of the Service to provide assistance to communities and persons therein in resolving disputes, disagreements, or difficulties relating to discriminatory practices based on race, color, or national origin which impair the rights of persons in such communities under the Constitution or laws of the United States or which affect or may affect interstate commerce. The Service may offer its services in cases of such disputes, disagreements, or difficulties whenever, in its judgment, peaceful relations among the citizens of the community involved are threatened thereby, and it may offer its services either upon its own motion or upon the request of an appropriate State or local official or other interested person.

SEC. 1003. (a) The Service shall, whenever possible, in performing its functions, seek and utilize the cooperation of appropriate State or local, public, or private agencies.

(b) The activities of all officers and employees of the Service in providing conciliation assistance shall be conducted in confidence and without publicity, and the Service shall hold confidential any information acquired in the regular performance of its duties upon the understanding that it would be so held. No officer or employee of the Service shall engage in the performance of investigative or prosecuting functions of any department or agency in any litigation arising out of a dispute in which he acted on behalf of the Service. Any officer or other employee of the Service, who shall make public in any manner whatever any information in violation of this subsection, shall be deemed guilty of a misdemeanor and, upon conviction thereof, shall be fined not more than $1,000 or imprisoned not more than one year.

SEC. 1004. Subject to the provisions of sections 205 and 1003(b), the Director shall, on or before January 31 of each year, submit to the Congress a report of the activities of the Service during the preceding fiscal year.

Roger L. Kemp

Title XI—Miscellaneous

SEC. 1101. In any proceeding for criminal contempt arising under title II, III, IV, V, VI, or VII of this Act, the accused, upon demand therefor, shall be entitled to a trial by jury, which shall conform as near as may be to the practice in criminal cases. Upon conviction, the accused shall not be fined more than $1,000 or imprisoned for more than six months.

This section shall not apply to contempts committed in the presence of the court, or so near thereto as to obstruct the administration of justice, nor to the misbehavior, misconduct, or disobedience of any officer of the court in respect to writs, orders, or process of the court. No person shall be convicted of criminal contempt hereunder unless the act or omission constituting such contempt shall have been intentional, as required in other cases of criminal contempt.

Nor shall anything herein be construed to deprive courts of their power, by civil contempt proceedings, without a jury, to secure compliance with or to prevent obstruction of, as distinguished from punishment for violations of, any lawful writ, process, order, rule, decree, or command of the court in accordance with the prevailing usages of law and equity, including the power of detention.

SEC. 1102. No person should be put twice in jeopardy under the laws of the United States for the same act or omission. For this reason, an acquittal or conviction in a prosecution for a specific crime under the laws of the United States shall bar a proceeding for criminal contempt, which is based upon the same act or omission and which arises under the provisions of this Act; and an acquittal or conviction in a proceeding for criminal contempt, which arises under the provisions of this Act, shall bar a prosecution for a specific crime under the laws of the United States based upon the same act or omission.

SEC. 1103. Nothing in this Act shall be construed to deny, impair, or otherwise affect any right or authority of the Attorney General or of the United States or any agency or officer thereof under existing law to institute or intervene in any action or proceeding.

SEC. 1104. Nothing contained in any title of this Act shall be construed as indicating an intent on the part of Congress to occupy the field in which any such title operates to the exclusion of State laws on the same subject matter, nor shall any provision of this Act be construed as invalidating any provision of State law unless such provision is inconsistent with any of the purposes of this Act, or any provision thereof.

SEC. 1105. There are hereby authorized to be appropriated such sums as are necessary to carry out the provisions of this Act.

SEC. 1106. If any provision of this Act or the application thereof to any person or circumstances is held invalid, the remainder of the Act and the application of the provision to other persons not similarly situated or to other circumstances shall not be affected thereby.

Approved July 2, 1964.

140

Voting Rights Act

(August 6, 1965)

United States Congress

The History[13]

This "act to enforce the fifteenth amendment to the Constitution" was signed into law 95 years after the amendment was ratified. In those years, African Americans in the South faced tremendous obstacles to voting, including poll taxes, literacy tests, and other bureaucratic restrictions to deny them the right to vote. They also risked harassment, intimidation, economic reprisals, and physical violence when they tried to register or vote. As a result, very few African Americans were registered voters, and they had very little, if any, political power, either locally or nationally.

In 1964, numerous demonstrations were held, and the considerable violence that erupted brought renewed attention to the issue of voting rights. The murder of voting-rights activists in Mississippi and the attack by state troopers on peaceful marchers in Selma, Alabama, gained national attention and persuaded President Johnson and Congress to initiate meaningful and effective national voting rights legislation. The combination of public revulsion to the violence and Johnson's political skills stimulated Congress to pass the voting rights bill on August 5, 1965.

The legislation, which President Johnson signed into law the next day, outlawed literacy tests and provided for the appointment of Federal examiners (with the power to register qualified citizens to vote) in those jurisdictions that were "covered" according to a formula provided in the statute. In addition, Section 5 of the act required covered jurisdictions to obtain "preclearance" from either the District Court for the District of Columbia or the U.S. Attorney General for any new voting practices and procedures. Section 2, which closely followed the language of the 15th amendment, applied a nationwide prohibition of the denial or abridgment of the right to vote on account of race or color. The use of poll taxes in national elections had been abolished by the 24th amendment (1964) to the Constitution; the Voting Rights Act directed the Attorney General to challenge the use of poll taxes in state and local elections. In *Harper v. Virginia State Board of Elections*, 383 U.S. 663 (1966), the Supreme Court held Virginia's, poll tax to be unconstitutional under the 14th amendment.

Because the Voting Rights Act of 1965 was the most significant statutory change in the relationship between the Federal and state governments in the area of voting since the Reconstruction period following the Civil War, it was immediately challenged in the courts. Between 1965 and

---

[13] Originally published as "Voting Rights Act (1965)," *America's Historical* Documents, The National Archives, U.S. National Archives and Records Administration, College Park, Maryland, 2008. For additional information see "Voting Rights Act (1965)," *America's Historical Documents*, U.S. National Archives and Records Administration, College Park, Maryland, 2008. This agency is listed in the *National Resource Directory* section of this volume.

1969, the Supreme Court issued several key decisions upholding the constitutionality of Section 5 and affirming the broad range of voting practices for which preclearance was required. [See *South Carolina v. Katzenbach*, 383 U.S. 301, 327–28 (1966) and *Allen v. State Board of Elections*, 393 U.S. 544 (1969)].

The law had an immediate impact. By the end of 1965, a quarter of a million new black voters had been registered, one-third by Federal examiners. By the end of 1966, only 4 out of the 13 southern states had fewer than 50 percent of African Americans registered to vote. The Voting Rights Act of 1965 was readopted and strengthened in 1970, 1975, and 1982.

The Document

Voting Rights Act

AN ACT To enforce the fifteenth amendment to the Constitution of the United States, and for other purposes.

Be it enacted by the Senate and House of Representatives of the United States of America in Congress [p*338] assembled, That this Act shall be known as the "Voting Rights Act of 1965."

SEC. 2. No voting qualification or prerequisite to voting, or standard, practice, or procedure shall be imposed or applied by any State or political subdivision to deny or abridge the right of any citizen of the United States to vote on account of race or color.

SEC. 3.

(a) Whenever the Attorney General institutes a proceeding under any statute to enforce the guarantees of the fifteenth amendment in any State or political subdivision the court shall authorize the appointment of Federal examiners by the United States Civil Service Commission in accordance with section 6 to serve for such period of time and for such political subdivisions as the court shall determine is appropriate to enforce the guarantees of the fifteenth amendment (1) as part of any interlocutory order if the court determines that the appointment of such examiners is necessary to enforce such guarantees or (2) as part of any final judgment if the court finds that violations of the fifteenth amendment justifying equitable relief have occurred in such State or subdivision: Provided, That the court need not authorize the appointment of examiners if any incidents of denial or abridgement of the right to vote on account of race or color (1) have been few in number and have been promptly and effectively corrected by State or local action, (2) the continuing effect of such incidents has been eliminated, and (3) there is no reasonable probability of their recurrence in the future. (b) If in a proceeding instituted by the Attorney General under any statute to enforce the guarantees of the fifteenth amendment in any State or political subdivision the court finds that a test or device has been used for the purpose or with the effect of denying or abridging the right of any citizen of the United States to vote on account of race or color, it shall suspend the use of [p*339] tests and devices in such State or political subdivisions as the court shall determine is appropriate and for such period as it deems necessary.

(c) If in any proceeding instituted by the Attorney General under any statute to enforce the guarantees of the fifteenth amendment in any State or political subdivision the court finds that violations of the fifteenth amendment justifying equitable relief have occurred within the territory of such State or political subdivision, the court, in addition to such relief as it may grant, shall retain jurisdiction for such period as it may deem appropriate and during such period no voting qualification or prerequisite to voting, or standard, practice, or procedure with respect to voting different from that in force or effect at the time the proceeding was commenced shall be enforced unless and until the court finds that such qualification, prerequisite, standard, practice, or procedure does not have the purpose and will not have the effect of denying or abridging the right to vote on account of race or color: Provided, That such qualification, prerequisite, standard, practice, or procedure may be enforced if the qualification, prerequisite, standard, practice, or procedure has been submitted by the chief legal officer or other appropriate official of such State or subdivision to the Attorney General and the Attorney General has not interposed an objection within sixty days after such submission, except that neither the court's finding nor the Attorney General's failure to object shall bar a subsequent action to enjoin enforcement of such qualification, prerequisite, standard, practice, or procedure.

SEC. 4. (a) To assure that the right of citizens of the United States to vote is not denied or abridged on account of race or color, no citizen shall be denied the right to vote in any Federal, State, or local election because of his failure to comply with any test or device in any State with respect to which the determinations have been [p*340] made under subsection (b) or in any political subdivision with respect to which such determinations have been made as a separate unit, unless the United States District Court for the District of Columbia in an action for a declaratory judgment brought by such State or subdivision against the United States has determined that no such test or device has been used during the five years preceding the filing of the action for the purpose or with the effect of denying or abridging the right to vote on account of race or color: Provided, That no such declaratory judgment shall issue with respect to any plaintiff for a period of five years after the entry of a final judgment of any court of the United States, other than the denial of a declaratory judgment under this section, whether entered prior to or after the enactment of this Act, determining that denials or abridgments of the right to vote on account of race or color through the use of such tests or devices have occurred anywhere in the territory of such plaintiff. An action pursuant to this subsection shall be heard and determined by a court of three judges in accordance with the provisions of section 2284 of title 28 of the United States Code and any appeal shall lie to the Supreme Court. The court shall retain jurisdiction of any action pursuant to this subsection for five years after judgment and shall reopen the action upon motion of the Attorney General alleging that a test or device has been used for the purpose or with the effect of denying or abridging the right to vote on account of race or color.

If the Attorney General determines that he has no reason to believe that any such test or device has been used during the five years preceding the filing of the action for the purpose or with the effect of denying or abridging the right to vote on account of race or color, he shall consent to the entry of such judgment.

(b) The provisions of subsection (a) shall apply in any State or in any political subdivision of a state which (1) the Attorney General determines maintained on November 1, 1964, any test or device, and with respect to which (2) the Director of the Census determines that less than 50 percentum of the persons of voting age residing therein were registered on November 1, 1964, or that less than 50 percentum of such persons voted in the presidential election of November 1964.

A determination or certification of the Attorney General or of the Director of the Census under this section or under section 6 or section 13 shall not be reviewable in any court and shall be effective upon publication in the Federal Register.

(c) The phrase "test or device" shall mean any requirement that a person as a prerequisite for voting or registration for voting (1) demonstrate the ability to read, write, understand, or interpret any matter, (2) demonstrate any educational achievement or his knowledge of any particular subject, (3) possess good moral character, or (4) prove his qualifications by the voucher of registered voters or members of any other class.

(d) For purposes of this section no State or political subdivision shall be determined to have engaged in the use of tests or devices for the purpose or with the effect of denying or abridging the right to vote on account of race or color if (1) incidents of such use have been few in number and have been promptly and effectively corrected by State or local action, (2) the continuing effect of such incidents has been eliminated, and (3) there is no reasonable probability of their recurrence in the future.

(e)(1) Congress hereby declares that to secure the rights under the fourteenth amendment of persons educated in American-flag schools in which the predominant [p*342] classroom language was other than English, it is necessary to prohibit the States from conditioning the right to vote of such persons on ability to read, write, understand, or interpret any matter in the English language. (2) No person who demonstrates that he has successfully completed the sixth primary grade in a public school in, or a private school accredited by, any State or territory, the District of Columbia, or the Commonwealth of Puerto Rico in which the predominant classroom language was other than English, shall be denied the right to vote in any Federal, State, or local election because of his inability to read, write, understand, or interpret any matter in the English language, except that, in States in which State law provides that a different level of education is presumptive of literacy, he shall demonstrate that he has successfully completed an equivalent level of education in a public school in, or a private school accredited by, any State or territory, the District of Columbia, or the Commonwealth of Puerto Rico in which the predominant classroom language was other than English.

SEC. 5. Whenever a State or political subdivision with respect to which the prohibitions set forth in section 4(a) are in effect shall enact or seek to administer any voting qualification or prerequisite to voting, or standard, practice, or procedure with respect to voting different from that in force or effect on November 1, 1964, such State or subdivision may institute an action in the United States District Court for the District of Columbia for a declaratory judgment that such qualification, prerequisite, standard, practice, or procedure does not have the purpose and will not have the effect of denying or abridging the right to vote on account of race or color, and unless and until the court enters such judgment no person shall be denied the right to vote for failure to comply with such qualification, prerequisite, standard, practice, [p*343] or procedure: Provided, That such qualification, prerequisite, standard, practice, or procedure may be enforced without such proceeding if the qualification, prerequisite, standard, practice, or procedure has been submitted by the chief legal officer or other appropriate official of such State or subdivision to the Attorney General and the Attorney General has not interposed an objection within sixty days after such submission, except that neither the Attorney General's failure to object nor a declaratory judgment entered under this section shall bar a subsequent action to enjoin enforcement of such qualification, prerequisite, standard, practice, or procedure. Any action under this section shall be heard and determined by a court of three judges in accordance with the provisions of section 2284 of title 28 of the United States Code and any appeal shall lie to the Supreme Court.

SEC. 6. Whenever (a) a court has authorized the appointment of examiners pursuant to the provisions of section 3(a), or (b) unless a declaratory judgment has been rendered under section 4(a), the Attorney General certifies with respect to any political subdivision named in, or included within the scope of, determinations made under section 4(b) that (1) he has received complaints in writing from twenty or more residents of such political subdivision alleging that they have been denied the right to vote under color of law on account of race or color, and that he believes such complaints to be meritorious, or (2) that, in his judgment (considering, among other factors, whether the ratio of nonwhite persons to white persons registered to vote within such subdivision appears to him to be reasonably attributable to violations of the fifteenth amendment or whether substantial evidence exists that bona fide efforts are being made within such subdivision to comply with the fifteenth amendment), the appointment of examiners is otherwise necessary to [p*344] enforce the guarantees of the fifteenth amendment, the Civil Service Commission shall appoint as many examiners for such subdivision as it may deem appropriate to prepare and maintain lists of persons eligible to vote in Federal, State, and local elections. Such examiners, hearing officers provided for in section 9(a), and other persons deemed necessary by the Commission to carry out the provisions and purposes of this Act shall be appointed, compensated, and separated without regard to the provisions of any statute administered by the Civil Service Commission, and service under this Act shall not be considered employment for the purposes of any statute administered by the Civil Service Commission, except the provisions of section 9 of the Act of August 2, 1939, as amended (5 U.S.C. 118i), prohibiting partisan political activity: Provided, That the Commission is authorized, after consulting the head of the appropriate department or agency, to designate suitable persons in the official service of the United States, with their consent, to serve in these positions. Examiners and hearing officers shall have the power to administer oaths.

SEC. 7.

(a) The examiners for each political subdivision shall, at such places as the Civil Service Commission shall by regulation designate, examine applicants concerning their qualifications for voting. An application to an examiner shall be in such form as the Commission may require and shall contain allegations that the applicant is not otherwise registered to vote.

(b) Any person whom the examiner finds, in accordance with instructions received under section 9(b), to have the qualifications prescribed by State law not inconsistent with the Constitution and laws of the United States shall promptly be placed on a list of eligible voters. A challenge to such listing may be made in accordance with section 9(a) and shall not be the basis for a prosecution under section 12 of this Act. The examiner [p*345] shall certify and transmit such list, and any supplements as appropriate, at least once a month, to the offices of the appropriate election officials, with copies to the Attorney General and the attorney general of the State, and any such lists and supplements thereto transmitted during the month shall be available for public inspection on the last business day of the month and, in any event, not later than the forty-fifth day prior to any election. The appropriate State or local election official shall place such names on the official voting list. Any person whose name appears on the examiner's list shall be entitled and allowed to vote in the election district of his residence unless and until the appropriate election officials shall have been notified that such person has been removed from such list in accordance with subsection (d): Provided, That no person shall be entitled to vote in any election by virtue of this Act unless his name shall have been certified and transmitted on such a list to the offices of the appropriate election officials at least forty-five days prior to such election.

(c) The examiner shall issue to each person whose name appears on such a list a certificate evidencing his eligibility to vote.

(d) A person whose name appears on such a list shall be removed therefrom by an examiner if (1) such person has been successfully challenged in accordance with the procedure prescribed in section 9, or (2) he has been determined by an examiner to have lost his eligibility to vote under State law not inconsistent with the Constitution and the laws of the United States.

Sec. 8. Whenever an examiner is serving under this Act in any political subdivision, the Civil Service Commission may assign, at the request of the Attorney General, one or more persons, who may be officers of the United States, (1) to enter and attend at any place for holding an election in such subdivision for the purpose [p*346] of observing whether persons who are entitled to vote are being permitted to vote, and (2) to enter and attend at any place for tabulating the votes cast at any election held in such subdivision for the purpose of observing whether votes cast by persons entitled to vote are being properly tabulated. Such persons so assigned shall report to an examiner appointed for such political subdivision, to the Attorney General, and if the appointment of examiners has been authorized pursuant to section 3(a), to the court.

SEC. 9.

(a) Any challenge to a listing on an eligibility list prepared by an examiner shall be heard and determined by a hearing officer appointed by and responsible to the Civil Service Commission and under such rules as the Commission shall by regulation prescribe. Such challenge shall be entertained only if filed at such office within the State as the Civil Service Commission shall by regulation designate, and within ten days after the listing of the challenged person is made available for public inspection, and if supported by (1) the affidavits of at least two persons having personal knowledge of the facts constituting grounds for the challenge, and (2) a certification that a copy of the challenge and affidavits have been served by mail or in person upon the person challenged at his place of residence set out in the application. Such challenge shall be determined within fifteen days after it has been filed. A petition for review of the decision of the hearing officer may be filed in the United States court of appeals for the circuit in which the person challenged resides within fifteen days after service of such decision by mail on the person petitioning for review but no decision of a hearing officer shall be reversed unless clearly erroneous. Any person listed shall be entitled and allowed to vote pending final determination by the hearing officer and by the court [p*347].

(b) The times, places, procedures, and form for application and listing pursuant to this Act and removals from the eligibility lists shall be prescribed by regulations promulgated by the Civil Service Commission and the Commission shall, after consultation with the Attorney General, instruct examiners concerning applicable State law not inconsistent with the Constitution and laws of the United States with respect to (1) the qualifications required for listing, and (2) loss of eligibility to vote.

(c) Upon the request of the applicant or the challenger or on its own motion the Civil Service Commission shall have the power to require by subpoena the attendance and testimony of witnesses and the production of documentary evidence relating to any matter pending before it under the authority of this section. In case of contumacy or refusal to obey a subpoena, any district court of the United States or the United States court of any territory or possession, or the District Court of the United States for the District of Columbia, within the jurisdiction of which said person guilty of contumacy or refusal to obey is found or resides or is domiciled or transacts business, or has appointed an agent for receipt of service of process, upon application by the Attorney General of the United States shall have jurisdiction to issue to such person an order requiring such person to appear before the Commission or a hearing officer, there to produce pertinent, relevant, and nonprivileged documentary evidence if so ordered, or there to give testimony touching the matter under investigation, and any failure to obey such order of the court may be punished by said court as a contempt thereof.

SEC. 10. (a) The Congress finds that the requirement of the payment of a poll tax as a precondition to voting (i) precludes persons of limited means from voting or imposes unreasonable financial hardship upon such persons [p*348] as a precondition to their exercise of the franchise, (ii) does not bear a reasonable relationship to any legitimate State interest in the conduct of elections, and (iii) in some areas has the purpose or effect of denying persons the right to vote because of race or color. Upon the basis of these findings, Congress declares that the constitutional right of citizens to vote is denied or abridged in some areas by the requirement of the payment of a poll tax as a precondition to voting. (b) In the exercise of the powers of Congress under section 5 of the fourteenth amendment and section 2 of the fifteenth amendment, the Attorney General is authorized and directed to institute forthwith in the name of the United States such actions, including actions against States or political subdivisions, for declaratory judgment or injunctive relief against the enforcement of any requirement of the payment of a poll tax as a precondition to voting, or substitute therefor enacted after November 1, 1964, as will be necessary to implement the declaration of subsection (a) and the purposes of this section.

(c) The district courts of the United States shall have jurisdiction of such actions which shall be heard and determined by a court of three judges in accordance with the provisions of section 2284 of title 28 of the United States Code and any appeal shall lie to the Supreme Court. It shall be the duty of the judges designated to hear the case to assign the case for hearing at the earliest practicable date, to participate in the hearing and determination thereof, and to cause the case to be in every way expedited.

(d) During the pendency of such actions, and thereafter if the courts, notwithstanding this action by the Congress, should declare the requirement of the payment of a poll tax to be constitutional, no citizen of the United States who is a resident of a State or political [p*349] subdivision with respect to which determinations have been made under subsection 4(b) and a declaratory judgment has not been entered under subsection 4(a), during the first year he becomes otherwise entitled to vote by reason of registration by State or local officials or listing by an examiner, shall be denied the right to vote for failure to pay a poll tax if he tenders payment of such tax for the current year to an examiner or to the appropriate State or local official at least forty-five days prior to election, whether or not such tender would be timely or adequate under State law. An examiner shall have authority to accept such payment from any person authorized by this Act to make an application for listing, and shall issue a receipt for such payment. The examiner shall transmit promptly any such poll tax payment to the office of the State or local official authorized to receive such payment under State law, together with the name and address of the applicant.

SEC. 11. (a) No person acting under color of law shall fail or refuse to permit any person to vote who is entitled to vote under any provision of this Act or is otherwise qualified to vote, or willfully fail or refuse to tabulate, count, and report such person's vote. (b) No person, whether acting under color of law or otherwise, shall intimidate, threaten, or coerce, or attempt to intimidate, threaten, or coerce any person for voting or attempting to vote, or intimidate, threaten, or coerce, or attempt to intimidate, threaten, or coerce any person for urging or aiding any person to vote or attempt to vote, or intimidate, threaten, or coerce any person for exercising any powers or duties under section 3(a), 6, 8, 9, 10, or 12(e).

(c) Whoever knowingly or willfully gives false information as to his name, address, or period of residence in the voting district for the purpose of establishing his eligibility to register or vote, or conspires with another [p*350] individual for the purpose of encouraging his false registration to vote or illegal voting, or pays or offers to pay or accepts payment either for registration to vote or for voting shall be fined not more than $10,000 or imprisoned not more than five years, or both: Provided, however, That this provision shall be applicable only to general, special, or primary elections held solely or in part for the purpose of selecting or electing any candidate for the office of President, Vice President, presidential elector, Member of the United States Senate, Member of the United States House of Representatives, or Delegates or Commissioners from the territories or possessions, or Resident Commissioner of the Commonwealth of Puerto Rico.

(d) Whoever, in any matter within the jurisdiction of an examiner or hearing officer knowingly and willfully falsifies or conceals a material fact, or makes any false, fictitious, or fraudulent statements or representations, or makes or uses any false writing or document knowing the same to contain any false, fictitious, or fraudulent statement or entry, shall be fined not more than $10,000 or imprisoned not more than five years, or both.

SEC. 12. (a) Whoever shall deprive or attempt to deprive any person of any right secured by section 2, 3, 4, 5, 7, or 10 or shall violate section 11(a) or (b), shall be fined not more than $5,000, or imprisoned not more than five years, or both. (b) Whoever, within a year following an election in a political subdivision in which an examiner has been appointed (1) destroys, defaces, mutilates, or otherwise alters the marking of a paper ballot which has been cast in such election, or (2) alters any official record of voting in such election tabulated from a voting machine or otherwise, shall be fined not more than $5,000, or imprisoned not more than five years, or both [p*351].

(c) Whoever conspires to violate the provisions of subsection (a) or (b) of this section, or interferes with any right secured by section 2, 3 4, 5, 7, 10, or 11(a) or (b) shall be fined not more than $5,000, or imprisoned not more than five years, or both.

(d) Whenever any person has engaged or there are reasonable grounds to believe that any person is about to engage in any act or practice prohibited by section 2, 3, 4, 5, 7, 10, 11, or subsection (b) of this section, the Attorney General may institute for the United States, or in the name of the United States, an action for preventive relief, including an application for a temporary or permanent injunction, restraining order, or other order, and including an order directed to the State and State or local election officials to require them (1) to permit persons listed under this Act to vote and (2) to count such votes.

(e) Whenever in any political subdivision in which there are examiners appointed pursuant to this Act any persons allege to such an examiner within forty-eight hours after the closing of the polls that notwithstanding (1) their listing under this Act or registration by an appropriate election official and (2) their eligibility to vote, they have not been permitted to vote in such election, the examiner shall forthwith notify the Attorney General if such allegations in his opinion appear to be well founded. Upon receipt of such notification, the Attorney General may forthwith file with the district court an application for an order providing for the marking, casting, and counting of the ballots of such persons and requiring the inclusion of their votes in the total vote before the results of such election shall be deemed final and any force or effect given thereto. The district court shall hear and determine such matters immediately after the filing of such application. The remedy provided [p*352] in this subsection shall not preclude any remedy available under State or Federal law.

(f) The district courts of the United States shall have jurisdiction of proceedings instituted pursuant to this section and shall exercise the same without regard to whether a person asserting rights under the provisions of this Act shall have exhausted any administrative or other remedies that may be provided by law.

SEC. 13. Listing procedures shall be terminated in any political subdivision of any State (a) with respect to examiners appointed pursuant to clause (b) of section 6 whenever the Attorney General notifies the Civil Service Commission, or whenever the District Court for the District of Columbia determines in an action for declaratory judgment brought by any political subdivision with respect to which the Director of the Census has determined that more than 50 percentum of the nonwhite persons of voting age residing therein are registered to vote, (1) that all persons listed by an examiner for such subdivision have been placed on the appropriate voting registration roll, and (2) that there is no longer reasonable cause to believe that persons will be deprived of or denied the right to vote on account of race or color in such subdivision, and (b), with respect to examiners appointed pursuant to section 3(a), upon order of the authorizing court. A political subdivision may petition the Attorney General for the termination of listing procedures under clause (a) of this section, and may petition the Attorney General to request the Director of the Census to take such survey or census as may be appropriate for the making of the determination provided for in this section. The District Court for the District of Columbia shall have jurisdiction to require such survey or census to be made by the Director of the Census and it shall require him to do so if it deems the Attorney [p*353] General's refusal to request such survey or census to be arbitrary or unreasonable. SEC. 14.

(a) All cases of criminal contempt arising under the provisions of this Act shall be governed by section 151 of the Civil Rights Act of 1957 (42 U.S.C. 1995). (b) No court other than the District Court for the District of Columbia or a court of appeals in any proceeding under section 9 shall have jurisdiction to issue any declaratory judgment pursuant to section 4 or section 5 or any restraining order or temporary or permanent injunction against the execution or enforcement of any provision of this Act or any action of any Federal officer or employee pursuant hereto.

(c)(1) The terms "vote" or "voting" shall include all action necessary to make a vote effective in any primary, special, or general election, including, but not limited to, registration, listing pursuant to this Act, or other action required by law prerequisite to voting, casting a ballot, and having such ballot counted properly and included in the appropriate totals of votes cast with respect to candidates for public or party office and propositions for which votes are received in an election. (2) The term "political subdivision" shall mean any county or parish, except that, where registration for voting is not conducted under the supervision of a county or parish, the term shall include any other subdivision of a State which conducts registration for voting.

(d) In any action for a declaratory judgment brought pursuant to section 4 or section 5 of this Act, subpoenas for witnesses who are required to attend the District Court for the District of Columbia may be served in any judicial district of the United States: Provided, That no writ of subpoena shall issue for witnesses without the District of Columbia at a greater distance than one hundred [p*314] miles from the place of holding court without the permission of the District Court for the District of Columbia being first had upon proper application and cause shown.

SEC. 15. Section 2004 of the Revised Statutes (42 U.S.C. 1971), as amended by section 131 of the Civil Rights Act of 1957 (71 Stat. 637), and amended by section 601 of the Civil Rights Act of 1960 (74 Stat. 90), and as further amended by section 101 of the Civil Rights Act of 1964 (78 Stat. 241), is further amended as follows:

(a) Delete the word "Federal" wherever it appears in subsections (a) and (c); (b) Repeal subsection (f) and designate the present subsections (g) and (h) as (f) and (g), respectively.

SEC. 16. The Attorney General and the Secretary of Defense, jointly, shall make a full and complete study to determine whether, under the laws or practices of any State or States, there are preconditions to voting, which might tend to result in discrimination against citizens serving in the Armed Forces of the United States seeking to vote. Such officials shall, jointly, make a report to the Congress not later than June 30, 1966, containing the results of such study, together with a list of any States in which such preconditions exist, and shall include in such report such recommendations for legislation as they deem advisable to prevent discrimination in voting against citizens serving in the Armed Forces of the United States.

SEC. 17. Nothing in this Act shall be construed to deny, impair, or otherwise adversely affect the right to vote of any person registered to vote under the law of any State or political subdivision.

SEC. 18. There are hereby authorized to be appropriated such sums as are necessary to carry out the provisions of this Act [p*355].

SEC 19. If any provision of this Act or the application thereof to any person or circumstances is held invalid, the remainder of the Act and the application of the provision to other persons not similarly situated or to other circumstances shall not be affected thereby.

Approved August 6, 1965.

APPENDICES

A. Glossary of Terms

Following is a list of terms commonly used to describe city, county, regional, state, and federal governments, and the actions taken by their public officials.

Abolish To do away with; to put an end to.

Act Legislation which has passed both Houses of Congress, approved by the President, or passed over his veto thus becoming law. Also used technically for a bill that has been passed by one House and engrossed.

Adjourn To stop or interrupt a meeting or session for a certain length of time.

Amendment A proposal by a Member (in committee or floor session of the respective Chamber) to alter the language or provisions of a bill or act. It is voted on in the same manner as a bill.

Appeal A request for a new hearing with a higher court.

Appellate Court A court which has the power to hear appeals and reverse court decisions.

Appointed Officials Public officials appointed by elected officials. These officials typically include an organization's top management staff (that is, chief executive and department managers).

Appointment An office or position for which one is chosen, not elected.

Appropriation A formal approval to draw funds from the Treasury for specific purposes. This may occur through an annual appropriations act, an urgent or supplemental appropriations act, a continuing resolution, or a permanent basis.

At-large Elections An election system where candidates are elected on a city-wide basis.

Authorization A law creating or sustaining a program, delegating power to implement it, and outlining its funding. Following authorization, an appropriation actually draws funds from the Treasury.

Bill A proposed law which is being considered for approval.

Bipartisanship Cooperation between Members of both political parties in addressing a particular issue or proposal. Bipartisan action usually results when party leaders agree that an issue is of sufficient national importance as to preclude normal considerations of partisan advantage.

Board of Supervisors Typical name for the members of a governing body of county.

Boards and Commissions Typical names given to advisory bodies, appointed by the members of a governing body, to advise them on matters of importance in one of the many functional areas of government.

Calendar A list of bills, resolutions, or other matters to be considered before committees or on the floor of either House of Congress.

Campaign An attempt to convince people to vote for someone for public office.

Candidate A person seeking to obtain an office or position.

Census An official count of the population.

Charter A written grant which establishes a local government corporation or other institution, and defines its purposes and privileges.

Checks and Balances System of government which maintains balance of power among the branches of the government. Sets limits on the power of each branch. Sets up ways for each branch to correct any misuses of power by the other branches.

Citizen Participation Strategies have greater legitimacy and are easier to implement politically when the citizens served by a governmental entity feel that their interests and issues have been properly addressed during the planning process.

City Council Typical name for the members of a governing body of a municipality.

City Manager The Chief Executive Officer of a municipality.

Civil Relating to the rights of individuals, such as property and personal freedoms. Also, court cases which are not criminal.

Civil Rights Rights which belong to a person because of his or her being a member of a particular society, for example, an American.

Combination Elections A hybrid election system where some candidates are elected on a city-wide basis, while other candidates are elected from a district, or ward.

Committee A group of people officially chosen to investigate or discuss a particular issue.

Compromise To settle differences by accepting less than what was wanted.

Constraint Limitation; restriction.

Contradict To conflict with; to oppose.

Controversial Relating to issues about which people have and express opposing views.

Cost/Benefit Analysis The relationship between economic benefits and cost associated with the operation of the department or program under study. The cost/benefit analysis may include both direct and indirect benefits and costs. Such analysis typically result in a payback period on initial investment.

Cost Center The smallest practical breakdown of expenditure and income into a grouping which will facilitate performance review, service evaluation, and the setting of priorities for particular activity or service area. Typically, it includes apportion of a single program within a department.

County Manager The Chief Executive Officer of a county government.

Cross Impact Analysis An analytical technique for identifying the various impacts of specific events or well-defined policy actions on other events. It explores whether the occurrence of one event or implementation of one policy is likely to inhibit, enhance, or have no effect on the occurrence of another event.

Criminal Relating to court cases in which a person has been accused of committing an action that is harmful to the public, such as murder or burglary.

Debate To discuss reasons for and against an issue or idea.

Delegate To grant or assign responsibility to another; to authorize a person or persons to represent the rest of the people.

Direct Democracy The people vote to make all of the decisions about their government.

Discrimination Being treated differently, usually worse, for some characteristic such as race, religion, national origin or sex. Discrimination is discouraged in the U.S.

District Elections An election system where candidates are elected from a district, or ward.

Econometric Model Forecasting technique that involves a system of interdependent regression equations that describe some sector of economic sales or profit activity. The parameters of the regression equations are usually estimated simultaneously. This technique better expresses the casualties involved than an ordinary regression equation.

Effectiveness Performing the right tasks correctly, consistent with a program's mission, goals, and objectives, or work plan. Relates to correctness and accuracy, not the efficiency of the program or tasks performed. Effectiveness alone is not an accurate measure of total productivity.

Efficiency Operating a program or performing work task economically. Relates to dollars spent or saved, not to the effectiveness of the program or task performed. Efficiency alone is not an accurate measure of total productivity.

Elected Officials Those public officials that hold elective office for a specified time period, typically called a term of office.

Environmental Scanning Process of identifying major environmental factors, events, or trends that impact, directly or indirectly, the organization and its internal operating systems. It is one of the initial steps in undertaking a strategic planning process.

Evaluation Systematic review of the mission, goals, objectives, and work plan for the organization and its various components. Evaluation occurs most frequently at the operational level by reviewing organizational objectives. The evaluation process typically results in the preparation of recommendation for needed adjustments.

Executive Person or group of persons responsible for governmental affairs and enforcement of laws.

Executive Director The title frequently used for the Chief Executive Officer of a regional government agency.

Exempt Free or excused from a requirement or duty.

External Environment All relevant elements or forces (for example, social, economic, political, and technological) external to, and having an impact on, the organization and its various components. Includes those forces that are not under the direct control of management.

Forecasting Techniques Methods (for example, qualitative, quantitative, and causal) used to project trends and predict future events or courses of action. Forecasting is an essential component of the strategic planning process. It may be used to analyze the external environment or to project organizational capabilities.

Foreign Policy The way a country treats and relates to the other countries of the world.

Forms of County Government Major forms include Commission, Commission-Administrator, and Council-Executive.

Forms of Municipal Government Major forms include Council-Manager, Mayor-Council, Commission, and Strong Mayor.

General Election A voting process involving most or all areas of the nation or state.

General Purpose Local Governments Includes cities and counties, since they both provide a wide range of services to the citizens they serve.

Gerrymandering Drawing of district lines to maximize the electoral advantage of political party or faction. The term was first used in 1812, when Elbridge Gerry was Governor of Massachusetts, to characterize the State redistricting plan.

Governor The Chief Executive Officer of a state government.

Hierarchical Ordered by rank or authority.

Hierarchy The order in which authority is ranked.

Impeach To charge a public official with committing a crime.

Inaugurate To place in office by a formal ceremony.

Influence The power to produce or cause an effect; to have an effect upon.

Inherent Rights Essential, basic rights.

Intergovernmental Relations The relationships between public officials at the various levels of government, most often dictated by legislation (e.g., grant requirements).

Internal Environment Relevant elements or forces (e.g., personnel, financial, communications, authority relationships, and management operating systems) internal to, and having an impact on, the operation of the organization and its various components. Includes those forces that are under the direct control of management.

Issue Trend, set of elements, or event which a group decides is important for policy-making purposes.

Issues Management Attempt to manage those issues that are important to an organization. These issues typically surface after the completion of an environmental scanning process, or other practice, leading to the identification of important issues. The issues identified should fall within the scope and purpose of the organization.

Jury A group of people chosen to hear a case in court. The *jury* makes a decision based upon the evidence.

Lame Duck Session A session of Congress meeting after elections have been held, but before the newly elected Congress has convened.

Law In municipal and county government this takes the form of an ordinance, which must be passed by majority vote of the governing body and published in a newspaper of general circulation.

Legislation The act or procedure of making laws; a law or laws made by such a procedure.

Levy To collect, a tax, for example.

Life-Cycle Analysis Involves an analysis and forecasting of new product or service growth rates based on S-curves. The phases of product or service acceptance by various groups are central to this analytical technique.

Line Personnel in those departments charged with responsibility for those functions necessary for the day-to-day performance of the organization. Includes those departments that directly produce goods and/or services to satisfy an organization's marketplace.

Line of Succession Order to succession.

Long-Range Planning Includes a planning process that commences with analyzing the internal organization and projecting current trends into the future for selected organizational components. This planning process may not include an assessment of an organization's external environment. It may be product or service oriented. This term should not be confused with strategic planning.

Management Consists basically of two types—strategic and operational. Strategic management is performed at the top of an organization's hierarchy; everything else is operational management. Operational management is organized along functional lines of responsibility. Strategic management sets direction for the organization, and operational management ensures that this direction is implemented.

Management Information System Integrated information system designed to provide strategic, tactical, and operational information to management. Usually involves periodic written or computer-generated reports which are timely, concise, and meaningful.

Management Operating System Formal system of linkages between different components of the organization by which the various departments communicate with each other and by which management directs the operation and receives information on its performance.

Mayor Typical name for the highest elective office in municipality.

Mission Statement of the role, or purpose, by which an organization plans to serve society. Mission statements may be set for different organizational components or departments. A department usually has only one mission statement.

Municipal The smallest unit of local government in the U.S.

Negotiate To discuss and then compromise on an issue to reach an agreement.

Nonprofit Organization Sometimes referred to as the third sector–the other two being the public and private sectors. Nonprofit organizations generally serve a public purpose and do not generate revenues beyond their operating expenses.

Objectives Tasks which are deemed necessary for an organization, or its components and departments, to achieve its goals. Several detailed objectives are typically set forth for each goal statement. Objectives include the operational implementation of goals.

Operational Issues Issues that relate to the internal operations of an organization such as finance, budgeting, personnel, and technology, to name a few. Operational issues may or may not relate to an organization's external environment and may not be of strategic importance to an organization.

Operational Management Tasks performed by line managers dealing with the operations of the organization. Operational managers may provide input into the formulation of strategic plans, but such plans are formulated by the planning group. Operational managers are key actors in implementing components of strategic plans.

Opponent Person who ran against others in an election for an office or position.

Opportunity Cost Cost of not taking a particular course of action. For example, if there are two issues and one is deemed to be strategic and the other is not, then the opportunity cost is the cost of not pursuing the course of action required for the nonstrategic issue. If the purchase of computers is a strategic issue, and the cost to purchase typewriters is not, then the cost of not acquiring the typewriters is an opportunity cost.

Override To nullify; to pass over.

Pardon To forgive a person for something he/she did wrong; to release or free a person from punishment.

Petition A formal request, usually written, for a right or benefit from a person or group with authority.

Philosophy The general beliefs, attitudes and ideas or theories of a person or group.

Platform The stated principles of a candidate for public office or a political party.

Policy Chosen course of action designed to significantly affect the organization's behavior in prescribed situations.

Political Action Committee (PAC) A group organized to promote its members' views on selected issues, usually through raising money that is contributed to the campaign funds of candidates who support the group's position.

President The Chief Executive Officer of the federal government organization.

Productivity Measure of performance that includes the requirements of both efficiency and effectiveness. Includes performing the program or work tasks correctly (effectively) and economically (efficiently).

Pro Tempore For the time being; temporarily.

Preliminary Introductory; something that comes before and is necessary to what follows.

Preside To hold the position of authority; to be in charge of a meeting or group.

Primary Election Election by which the candidate who will represent a particular political party is chosen.

Ratification Two uses of this term are: (1) the act of approval of a proposed constitutional amendment by the legislatures of the States; (2) the Senate process of advice and consent to treaties negotiated by the President.

Ratify To approve or confirm formally; to make valid and binding.

Redistricting The process within the States of redrawing legislative district boundaries to reflect population changes following the decennial census.

Regional Government A multi-jurisdictional agency that includes any combination of cities and counties, and is usually sub-state in nature. Only a few regional governments involve more than one state.

Regulation Rule or order which controls actions and procedures.

Repeal To take back or recall, usually a law.

Representative Democracy The people choose or elect officials to make decisions for them about their government. On some issues, however, the people vote, rather than their representatives.

Republican Democratic; representative.

Resolution A legislative act without the force of law, such as action taken to adopt a policy or to modify an existing program.

Ruling The official decision of a court on the case being tried.

Sentence Judgment or decision; usually a decision on the punishment for a person convicted of a crime.

Special Purpose Local Governments Includes special districts, which perform a single public service or function (e.g., water, sewer, and transportation districts, to name a few).

Staff Personnel in those departments designed to serve the operating components, or line departments, of an organization (e.g., personnel, finance, general services, purchasing, etc.).

Stakeholder Those individuals, groups, and outside parties that either affect or who are affected by the organization. Examples include constituents, special-interest groups, suppliers, unions, employees, policy-makers, and advisory bodies, to name a few. In any strategic planning process these entities must either be involved or consulted so that their views are given consideration during the planning process.

Strategic Issues Issues included in a strategic plan which are deemed important to the organization and its future performance. These issues may be either internal or external to the organization itself. Typically, external issues are more difficult to manage than internal issues, due to the limited degree of control exercised by public organizations over their outside environment.

Strategic Management Involves setting direction for the organization and typically performed by elected and appointed officials, or some combination of these individuals, once a strategic plan is approved for implementation. While the strategic plan is approved by elected officials, top management is responsible for its administrative implementation.

Strategic Vision Explicit, shared understanding of the nature and purpose of the organization. It specifies what the organization is and should be rather than what it does operationally. The strategic vision is contained within an organization's strategy statement.

Strategy General direction set for the organization and its various components to achieve a desired state in the future. Strategy results from the detailed planning process that assesses the external and internal environment of an organization and results in a work plan that includes mission statements to direct the goals and objectives of the organization.

Structure Segmentation of work into components, typically organized around those goods and services produced, the formal lines of authority and communication between these components, and the information that flows between these communication and authority relationships.

Succession Order in which one person follows another in replacing a person in an office or position.

Table To postpone or delay making a decision on an issue or law.

Time Horizon A timespan included in a plan, or planning document, varies depending on the type of plan being developed. Strategic plans typically have a five or ten year, sometimes longer, time horizon. Operational plans, on the other hand, frequently project a three to five-year timespan into the future.

Unconstitutional In conflict with a constitution.

Veto Power of the head of the executive branch to keep a bill from becoming law.

Editor's Note: Some of the above terms were taken from *U.S. Government Structure* (1987), and *Our American Government* (1993), U.S. Government Printing Office, Washington, D.C. copies of these books may be obtained from the U.S. Government Printing Office, P.O. Box 371954, Pittsburgh, Pennsylvania 15250-7954, or may be ordered over the internet from GPO's online bookstore (http://bookstore.gpo.gov).

B. Local Government Historical Document

(Mecklenburg County was the first local government in America to declare its Independence from Great Britain)

The Mecklenburg Resolution[1]
(May 20, 1775)

I. *Resolved*: That whosoever directly or indirectly abets, or in any way, form, or manner countenances the unchartered and dangerous invasion of our rights, as claimed by Great Britain, is an enemy to this country–to America–and to the inherent and inalienable rights of man.

II. *Resolved*: That we do hereby declare ourselves a free and independent people; are, and of right ought to be a sovereign and self-governing association, under the control of no power, other than that of our God and the General Government of the Congress: To the maintenance of which Independence was solemnly pledge to each other our mutual co-operation, our Lives, our Fortunes, and our most Sacred Honor.

III. *Resolved*: That as we acknowledge the existence and control of no law or legal officer, civil or military, within this county, we do hereby ordain and adopt as a rule of life, all, each, and every one of our former laws, wherein, nevertheless, the Crown of Great Britain never can be considered as holding rights, privileges, or authorities therein.

IV. *Resolved*: That all, each, and every Military Officer in this country is hereby reinstated in his former command and authority, he acting to their regulations, and that every Member present of this Delegation, shall henceforth be a Civil Officer, viz: a Justice of the Peace, in the character of a Committee Man, to issue process, hear and determine all matters of controversy, according to said adopted laws, and to preserve Peace, Union, and Harmony in said county, to use exertion to spread the Love of Country and Fire of Freedom throughout America, until a more general and organized government be established in this Province

ABRAHAM ALEXANDER, *chairman*.
JOHN MCKNITT ALEXANDER, *Secretary*

REFERENCE

1. This declaration of independence (with supplementary set of resolutions establishing a form of government) was adopted (as it is claimed) by a convention of delegates from different sections of Mecklenburg County, which assembled at Charlotte May 20, 1775.

C. United States Voting Rights History

(Year, Legislation, Impact)

1776	*Declaration of Independence*	Right to vote during the colonial and Revolutionary and Revolutionary periods is restricted to property owners.
1787	*United States Constitution*	States are given the power to regulate their own voting rights.
1856	*State Legislation*	North Carolina is the last state to remove property ownership as a requirement for voting.
1868	*14ᵗʰ Amendment to the U.S. Constitution*	Citizenship is granted to all former slaves. Voters are still defined as male. Voting regulations are still a right of the states.
1870	*15ᵗʰ Amendment to the U.S. Constitution*	It is now law that the right to vote cannot be denied by the federal or state governments based on race.
1887	*Daws Act*	Citizenship is granted to Native Americans who give up their Tribal affiliations.
1890	*State Constitution*	Wyoming is admitted to statehood and becomes the first state to Legislate voting rights for women in its state constitution.
1913	*17ᵗʰ Amendment to the U. S. Constitution*	New law that allows citizens to vote for members of the U.S. Senate, instead of the past practice of having them elected by State Legislatures.
1915	*U.S. Supreme Court Decision*	The U.S. Supreme Court outlawed, in *Guinn v. United States* (Oklahoma), literacy tests for federal elections. The court Ruled that this practice was in violation of the 15ᵗʰ Amendment To the U.S. Constitution.

1920	*19th Amendment to the U.S. Constitution*	Women were given the right to vote in both state and federal elections.
1924	*Indian Citizenship*	This law granted all Native Americans the rights of citizenship, Including the right to vote in federal elections.
1944	*U.S. Supreme Court Decision*	The U.S. Supreme Court outlawed, in *Smith v. Allright* (Texas), "white primaries" in Texas and other States. The court ruled that this practice was in violation of the 15th Amendment to the U.S. Constitution.
1957	*Civil Rights Act*	The first law to implement the 15th Amendment to the U.S. Constitution is passed. This law established the Civil Rights Commission, which formally investigates complaints of voter Discrimination made by citizens.
1960	*U.S. Supreme Court Decision*	The U.S. Supreme Court, in *Gomillion v. Lightfoot* (Alabama), outlawed the use of "gerrymandering" in election practices. This practice includes boundary determination (or Redistricting) changes being made for electoral advantage.
1961	*23rd Amendment to the U.S. Constitution*	Citizens of Washington, DC, are given the right to vote in presidential elections.
1964	*24th Amendment to the U.S. Constitution*	The right for citizens to vote in federal elections cannot be denied for failure to pay a poll tax.
1965	*Voting Rights Act*	This law forbids states from imposing discriminatory restrictions On the voting right of citizens, and provides mechanisms to The federal government for the enforcement of this law. This Act was expanded and renewed in 1970, 1975, 1982, and 2006.

| 1966 | *U.S. Supreme Court Decision* | The U.S. Supreme Court, in *Harper v. Virginia Board of Education* (Virginia), eliminated the poll tax as a qualification for voting in any election. This practice was found to be in Violation of the 24th Amendment to the U.S. Constitution. |

| 1966 | *U.S. Supreme Court Decision* | The U.S. Supreme Court, in *South Carolina v. Katzenbach* (South Carolina), upheld the legality of the Voting Rights Act of 1965. |

| 1970 | *U.S. Supreme Court Decision* | The U.S. Supreme Court, in *Oregon v. Mitchell* (Oregon), upheld the ban on the use of literacy tests as a requirement for voting. This ban was made permanent in the 1975 Amendment to the Voting Rights Act. |

| 1971 | *26th Amendment to the U.S. Constitution* | The national legal voting age is reduced from 21 years old to 18 years old. |

| 1972 | *U.S. Supreme Court Decision* | The U.S. Supreme Court, in *Dunn v. Blumstein* (Tennessee), ruled that lengthy residency requirements for voting in state and local elections are unconstitutional, and suggested a 30-day Residency period as being adequate. |

| 1975 | *Amendments to the Voting Rights Act* | Mandated that certain voting materials must be printed in languages besides English so that people who do not read English can participate in the voting process. |

| 1993 | *National Voter Registration Act* | Attempts to increase the number of eligible citizens who register to vote by making registration available at each state's Department of Motor Vehicles, as well as public assistance and disability agencies. |

| 2002 | *Help America Vote Act* | Law requires that states comply withy federal mandates for Provisional ballots; disability access; centralized, computerized voting lists; electronic voting; and the requirement that first-time voters present identification before they can vote. |

2003   *Federal Voting Standards And* Requires all states to streamline their voter
        Procedures Act   registration process, voting practices, and election
                                             procedures.

NOTE

For additional information concerning these documents, and related information, please refer to the *Federal Election Commission*, which is listed in the *National Resource Directory* section of this volume.

D. National Resource Directory

(organized by topics for the public, nonprofit, and educational sectors)

Civic Education

Ackerman Center for Democratic Citizenship
(http://www.education/purdue.edu/ackerman-center)

American Democracy Project
(http://www.aascu.org/programs/adp/)

Bill of Rights Institute
(http://www.civiced.org/)

Center for Civic Education
(http://www.civiced.org/)

Center for Youth Citizenship
(http://www.youthcitizenship.org/)

Civic Education Project
(http://www.civiceducationproject.org/)

Civnet
(http://civnet.org/)

Constitutional Rights Foundation
(http://www.crf-usa.org/)

Kellogg Foundation
(http://www.wkkf.org/)

Civic Renewal Initiative
(http://www.ncoc.org/)

National Endowment for Democracy
(http://www.ned.org/)

National Institute for Citizens Education and Law
(https://eric.ed.gov)

Civil Rights and Civil Liberties

American Civil Liberties Union
(http://www.aclu.org/)

Citizens Commission on Civil Rights
(http://www.cccr.org/)

Constitution Society
(http://www.constitution.org/)

Freedom Forum
(http://www.freedomforum.org/)

Judicial Watch
(http://www.judicialwatch.org/)

League of Women Voters
(http://www.lwv.org/)

National Coalition again Censorship
(http://www.ncac.org/)

Project Vote Smart
(http://www.vote-smart.org/)

Historical

Center for the Study of Federalism
(http://www.federalism.org/)

Center for the Study of the Presidency
(http://www.thepresidency.org/)

Constitutional Facts
(http://www.constitutionfacts.com/)

Freedom Foundation at Valley Forge
(http://www.ffvf.org/)

National Constitution Center
(http://www.constitutioncenter.org/)

Supreme Court Historical Society
(http://www.supremecourthistory.org/)

The Avalon Project
(http://avalon.law.yale.edu/)

White House Historical Association
(http://www.whitehousehistory.org/)

Political Parties

Democratic National Committee
(http://www.democrats.org/)

Green Party of North America
(http://www.greens.org/)

Libertarian Party
(http://www.lp.org/)

Natural Law Party
(http://www.natural-law.org/)

Reform Party
(http://www.reformparty.org/)

Republican National Committee
(http://www.gop.com/)

Socialist Party
(http://www.socialist.org/)

Professional Associations
(http://www.abanet.org/)

American Planning Association
(http://www.planning.org/)

American Political Science Association
(http://www.apsanet.org/)

American Society for Public Administration
(http://www.aspanet.org/)

Association for Metropolitan Planning Organizations
(http://www.ampo.org/)

Public Policy

Association for Public Policy Analysis and Management
(http://www.appam.org/)

Center for Policy Alternatives
(http://www.cfpa.org/)

Center for Public Integrity
(http://www.publicintegrity.org/)

Common Cause
(http://www.commoncause.org/)

National Center for Policy Analysis
(http://www.ncpa.org/)

National Center for Public Policy Research
(http://www.nationalcenter.org/)

National Legal Center for Public Interest
(http://www.nlcpi.org/)

Pew Research Center
(http://pewresearch.org/)

State and Local Government

Council of State Governments
(http://www.csg.org/)

International City/County Management Association
(http://www.icma.org/)

Local Government Commission
(http://www.lgc.org/)

Meyner Center for the study of State and Local Government
(http://meynercenter.lafayette.edu/)

National Association of Counties
(http://www.naco.org/)

National Association of Regional Councils
(http://www.narc.org/)

National Association of Towns and Townships
(http://natat.org/)

National Center for State Courts
(http://www.ncsc.org/)

National Civic League
(http://www.ncl.org/)

National Conference of State Legislatures
(http://www.ncsl.org/)

National Governors Association
(http://www.nga.org/)

National League of Cities
(http://www.nlc.org/)

Secretary of State/State of Connecticut
(http://www.sots.ct.gov/)

U.S. Conference of Mayors
(http://www.usmayors.org/)

State Supreme Judicial Court
Commonwealth of Massachusetts
(http://www.mass.gov/courts/sjcl)

U.S. Government

Federal Communications Commission
(http://www.fcc.gov/)

Federal Elections Commission
(http://www.fec.gov/)

Federal Judicial Center
(http://www.fjc.gov/)

Federal Judiciary Homepage
(http://www.uscourts.gov/)

Library of Congress
(http://lcweb.loc.gov/)

National Endowment for the Humanities
(http://www.neh.gov/)

Thomas Legislative Information
(http://www.congress.gov/)

U.S. Census Bureau
(http://www.census.gov/)

U.S. Department of State
(http://www.state.gov)

U.S. Department of the Interior
(http://www.doi.gov/)

U.S. House of Representatives
(http://www.house.gov/)

U.S. National Archives and Records Administration
(http://www.archives.gov/)

U.S. Senate
(http://www.senate.gov/)

U.S. Supreme Court
(http://www.supremecourtus.gov/)

White House
(http://www.whitehouse.gov/)

Others

Brookings Institution
(http://www.Brookings.edu/)

Civics & The Future of Democracy
(http://futureofcivics.theatlantic.com)

Heritage Foundation
(http://www.heritage.org/)

National Humanities Institute
(http://www.nhinet.org/)

National Taxpayers Union
(http://www.ntu.org/)

National Urban League
(http://www.nul.org/)

Smithsonian Institution
(http://www.si.edu/)

Street Law, Inc.
(http://www.streetlaw.org/)

Supreme Court Decisions
(http://supct.law.cornell.edu/supct/)

United Kingdom Parliamentary Archives
(http://www.parliament.uk/archives/)

Urban Institute
(http://www.urban.org/)

Wikipedia Encyclopedia
(http://www.wikipedia.org/)

NOTE

Some professional association are listed under headings that fit their primary mission. Those that don't fit into one of the general topics are listed above under "others."

E. State Municipal League Directory

Most states have a municipal league, which serves as a valuable source of information about city government innovations and programs. Additional information on eminent domain is available from the following state municipal league websites:

Alabama League of Municipalities
(http://www.alalm.org/)

Alaska Municipal League
(http://www.akml.org/)

League of Arizona Cities and Towns
(http://www.azleague.org/)

Arkansas Municipal League
(http://www.arml.org/)

League of California Cities
(http://www.cacities.org/)

Colorado Municipal League
(http://www.cml.org/)

Connecticut Conference of Municipalities
(http://www.ccm-ct.org/)

Delaware League of Local Governments
(http://www.ipa.udel.edu/localgovt/dllg/)

Florida League of Cities
(http://www.flcities.com/)

Georgia Municipal Association
(http://www.gmanet.com/)

Association of Idaho Cities
(http://www.idahocities.org/)

Illinois Municipal League
(http://www.iml.org/)

Indiana Association of Cities and Towns
(http://www.citiesandtowns.org/)

Iowa League of Cities
(http://www.iowaleague.org/)

League of Kansas Municipalities
(http://www.lkm.org/)

Kentucky League of Cities, Inc.
(http://www.klc.org/)

Louisiana Municipal Association
(http://www.lma.org/)

Maine Municipal Association
(http://www.memun.org/)

Maryland Municipal League
(http://www.mdmunicipal.org/)

Massachusetts Municipal Association
(http://www.mma.org/)

Michigan Municipal League
(http://www.mml.org/)

League of Minnesota Cities
(http://www.lmc.org/)

Mississippi Municipal League
(http://www.mmlonline.com/)

Missouri Municipal League
(http://www.mocities.com/)

Montana League of Cities and Towns
(http://www.mtleague.org/)

League of Nebraska Municipalities
(http://www.lonm.org/)

Nevada League of Cities and Municipalities
(http://www.nvleague.org/)

New Hampshire Municipal Association
(http://www.nhmunicipal.org/)

New Jersey State League of Municipalities
(http://www.njlm.org/)

New Mexico Municipal League
(www.nmml.org/)

New York State Conference of Mayors and Municipal Officials
(http://www.nycom.org/)

North Carolina League of Municipalities
(http://www.nclm.org/)

North Dakota League of Cities
(http://www.ndlc.org/)

Ohio Municipal League
(http://www.omlohio.org/)

Oklahoma Municipal League
(http://www.oml.org/)

League of Oregon Cities
(http://www.orcities.org/)

Pennsylvania Municipal League
(http://www.pml.org/)

Rhode Island League of Cities And Towns
(http://www.rileague.org/)

Municipal Association of South Carolina
(http://www.masc.sc/)

South Dakota Municipal League
(http://www.sdmunicipalleague.org/)

Tennessee Municipal League
(http://www.tmll.org/)

Texas Municipal League
(http://www.tml.org/)

Utah League of Cities and Towns
(http://www.ulct.org/)

Vermont League of Cities and Towns
(http://www.vlct.org/)

Virginia Municipal League
(http://www.vml.org/)

Association of Washington Cities
(http://www.awcnet.org/)

West Virginia Municipal League
(http://www.wvml.org/)

League of Wisconsin Municipalities
(http://www.lwm-info.org/)

Wyoming Association of Municipalities
(http://www.wyomuni.org/)

F. State Library Directory

Most state libraries have copies of state laws, both proposed and adopted in an on-line database. Many states also have copies of the various laws adopted in those cities and towns within their jurisdictions. They are an excellent resource for eminent domain.

Alabama
Alabama Department of Archives & History,
(http://archives.state.al.us/)

Alabama Public Library Services
(http://statelibrary.alabama.gov/)

Alaska
Alaska State Library
(http://www.library.alaska.gov/)

Arizona
Arizona Department of Library, Archives and Public Records
(http://www.azlibrary.gov/)

Arkansas
Arkansas State Library
(http://www.asl.lib.ar.us/)

California
California State Library
(http://www.library.ca.gov/)

Colorado
Colorado State Library and Adult Education Office
(http://www.cde.state.co.us/cdelib/)

Colorado Virtual Library
(http://www.coloradovirtuallibrary.org/)

Connecticut
Connecticut State Library
(http://www.ctstatelibrary.org/)

Delaware
Delaware Library Catalog Consortium
(http://lib.de.us/about-us/about-dlc/)

Delaware Division of Libraries
(http://www.libraries.delaware.gov/)

District of Columbia
District of Columbia Public Library
(http://www.dclibrary.org/)

Florida
State Library and Archives of Florida
(https://www.dos.myflorida.com/library-archives)

Georgia
Office of Public Library Services
(http://www.georgialibraries.org/)

Hawaii
Hawaii State Public Library System
(http://www.librarieshawaii.org/)

Idaho
Idaho Commission for Libraries
(http://libraries.idaho.gov/)

Illinois
Illinois State Library
(https://cyberdriveillinois.com/departments/library/)

Indiana
Indiana State Library
(http://www.in.gov/library/)

Iowa
State Library of Iowa
(http://www.statelibraryofiowa.org/)

Kansas
Kansas State Library
(http://www.kslib.info/)

Kentucky
Kentucky Department for Libraries and Archives
(http://www.kdla.ky.gov/)

Louisiana
State Library of Louisiana
(http://www.state.lib.la.us/)

Maine
Maine State Library
(http://www.state.me.us/msl.)

Maryland
Sailor: Maryland's Public Information Network
(http://www.sailor.lib.md.us/)

Massachusetts
Massachusetts Board of Library Commissioners
(http://mblc.state.ma.us/)

Michigan
Library of Michigan
(http://www.michigan.gov/libraryofmichigan)

Minnesota
State Government Libraries
(http://www.libraries.state.mn.us/)

Mississippi
Mississippi Library Commission
(http://www.mlc.lib.ms.us/)

Missouri
Missouri State Library
(http://www.sos.mo.gov/library/)

Montana
Montana State Library
(http://www.home.msl.mt.gov/)

Nebraska
Nebraska Library Commission
(http://www.nlc.state.ne.us/)

Nevada
Nevada State Library and Archives
(http://www.nsladigitalcollections.org)

New Hampshire
New Hampshire State Library
(http://www.nh.gov/nhsl/)

New Jersey
The New Jersey State Library
(http://www.njstatelib.org/)

New Mexico
New Mexico State Library
(http://www.nmstatelibrary.org/)

New York
The New York State Library
(http://www.nysl.nysed.gov/)

New York State Archives
(http://www.archives.nysed.gov/)

North Carolina
State Library of North Carolina
(https://statelibrary.ncdcr.gov/)

North Dakota
North Dakota State Library
(http://www.library.nd.gov/)

Ohio
State Library of Ohio
(http://www.www.library.ohio.gov/)

Oklahoma
Oklahoma Department of Libraries
(http://www.odl.state.ok.us/)

Oregon
Oregon State Library
(http://oregon.gov/OSL/)

Pennsylvania
State Library of Pennsylvania
(http://www.statelibrary.pa.gov/)

Rhode Island
Office of Library and Information Services
(http://www.olis.ri.gov/)

South Carolina
South Carolina State Library
(http://www.statelibrary.sc.gov/)

South Dakota
South Dakota State Library
(http://library.sd.gov/)

Tennessee
Tennessee State Library & Archives
(http://www.tennessee.gov/tsla/)

Texas
Texas State Library and Archives Commission
(http://www.tsl.state.tx.us/)

Utah
Utah State Library
(https://library.utah.gov/)

Vermont
Vermont Department of Libraries
(http://libraries.vermont.gov/)

Virginia
The Library of Virginia
(http://www.lva.virginia.gov/)

Washington
Washington State Library
(http://www.secstate.wa.gov/library/)

West Virginia
West Virginia Library Commission
(http://wvlc.lib.wv.us/)

West Virginia Archives and History
(http://www.wvculture.org/history/)

Wisconsin
Wisconsin Department of Public Instruction:
Division for Libraries, Technology, and Community Learning
(http://www.dpi.wi.gov/dltcl/)

Wyoming
Wyoming State Library
(http://www.library.wyo.gov/)

G. Books by Roger L. Kemp

(as author, contributing author, and editor)

(1) Roger L Kemp, ***Coping with Proposition 13***, Lexington Books, D.C. Heath and Company, Lexington, MA, and Toronto, Canada (1980)

(2) Roger L. Kemp, "The Administration of Scarcity: Managing Government in Hard Times," ***Conferencia De Las Grandes Ciudades De Las America***, Interamerican Foundation of Cities, San Juan, Puerto Rico (1983)

(3) Roger L. Kemp, ***Cutback Management: A trinationol Perspective***, Transaction Books, New Brunswick, NJ, and London, England (1983)

(4) Roger L. Kemp, ***Research in Urban Policy: Coping with Urban Austerity***, JAI Press, Inc., Greenwich, CT, and London, England (1985)

(5) Roger L. Kemp, ***America's Infrastructure: Problems and Prospects***, The Interstate Printers and Publishers, Danville, IL (1986)

(6) Roger L. Kemp, ***Coping with Proposition 13: Strategies for Hard Times***, Robert E. Krieger Publishing Company, Malabar, FL (1988)

(7) Roger L. Kemp, ***America's Cities: Strategic Planning for the Future***, The Interstate Printers and Publishers, Danville, IL (1988)

(8) Roger L. Kemp, ***The Hidden Wealth of Cities: Policy and Productivity Methods for American Local Governments***, JAI Press, Inc., Greenwich, CT and London, England (1989)

(9) Roger L. Kemp, ***Strategic Planning in Local Government: A Casebook***, Planners Press, American Planning Association, Chicago, IL, and Washington, D.C. (1992)

(10) Roger L. Kemp, ***Strategic Planning for Local Government***, International City/County Management Association, Washington, D.C. (1993)

(11) Roger L. Kemp, ***America's Cities: Problems and Prospects***, Avebury Press, Alershot, England (1995)

(12) Roger L. Kemp, ***Helping Business – The Library's Role in Community Economic Development, A How-To-D-It Manual***, Neal Schuman Publishers, Inc., New York, NY, and London, England (1997)

(13) Roger L. Kemp, ***Homeland Security: Best Practices for Local Government***, 1st Edition, International City/County Management Association, Washington, D.C. (2003)

(14) Roger L Kemp, ***Cities and the Arts: A handbook for Renewal***, McFarland & Company, Inc., Jefferson, NC (2004)

(15) Roger L. Kemp, ***Homeland Security Handbook for Citizen and Public Officials***, McFarland & Company, Inc., Jefferson, NC (2006)

(16) Roger L. Kemp, ***Main Street Renewal: A Handbook for Citizens and Public Officials***, McFarland & Company, Inc., Jefferson, NC (2006, 2000)

(17) Roger L. Kemp, *Local Government Election Practices: A Handbook for Public Officials and Citizens*, McFarland & Company, Inc., Jefferson, NC (2006, 1999)

(18) Roger L. Kemp, *Cities and Nature: A Handbook for Renewal*, McFarland & Company, Inc., Jefferson, NC (2006)

(19) Roger L. Kemp, *Emergency Management and Homeland Security*, International City/County Management Association, Washington, D.C. (2006)

(20) Roger L. Kemp, *The Inner City: A Handbook for Renewal*, McFarland & Company, Inc., Jefferson, NC (2007, 2001)

(21) Roger L. Kemp, *Privatization: The Provision of Public Services by the Private Sector*, McFarland & Company, Inc., Jefferson, NC (2007, 1991)

(22) Roger L. Kemp, *Community Renewal through Municipal Investment: A Handbook for Citizens and Public Officials*, McFarland & Company, Inc., Jefferson, NC (2007, 2003)

(23) Roger L. Kemp, *How American Government Works: A Handbook on City, County, Regional, State, and Federal Operations*, McFarland & Company, Inc., Jefferson, NC (2007, 2002)

(24) Roger L. Kemp, *Regional Government Innovations: A Handbook for Citizens and Public Officials*, McFarland & Company, Inc., Jefferson, NC (2007, 2003)

(25) (25) Roger L. Kemp, *Economic Development in Local Government: A Handbook for Public Officials and Citizens*, McFarland & Company, Inc.., Jefferson, NC (2007, 1995)

(26) Roger L. Kemp, *Model Practices for Municipal Governments*, Connecticut Town and City Management Association, University of Connecticut, West Hartford, CT (2007)

(27) Roger L. Kemp, *Managing America's Cities: A Handbook for Local Government Productivity*, McFarland & Company, Inc., Jefferson, NC (2007, 1998)

(28) Roger L. Kemp, *Model Government Charters: A City, County, Regional, State, and Federal Handbook*, McFarland & Company, Inc., Jefferson, NC (2007, 2003)

(29) Roger L. Kemp, *Forms of Local Government: A Handbook on City, County and Regional Options*, McFarland & Company, Inc., Jefferson, NC (2007, 1999)

(30) Roger L. Kemp, *Cities and Cars: A Handbook of Best Practices*, McFarland & Company, Inc., Jefferson, NC (2007)

(31) Roger L. Kemp, *Homeland Security for the Private Sector: A Handbook*, McFarland & Company, Inc., Jefferson, NC (2007)

(32) Roger L. Kemp, *Strategic Planning for Local Government: A Handbook for Officials and Citizens*, McFarland & Company, Inc., Jefferson, NC (2008, 1993)

(33) Roger L. Kemp, *Museums, Libraries and Urban Vitality: A Handbook*, McFarland & Company, Inc., Jefferson, NC (2008)

(34) Roger L. Kemp, *Cities and Growth: A Policy Handbook*, McFarland & Company, Inc., Jefferson, NC (2008)

(35) Roger L. Kemp, *Cities and Sports Stadiums: A Planning Handbook*, McFarland & Company, Inc., Jefferson, NC (2009)

(36) Roger L. Kemp, *Cities and Water: A Handbook for Planning*, McFarland & Company, Inc., Jefferson, NC (2009)

(37) Roger L. Kemp, *Homeland Security: Best Practices for Local Government*, 2nd Edition, International city/County Management Association, Washington, D.C. (2010)

(38) Roger L. Kemp, *Cities and Adult Businesses: A Handbook for Regulatory Planning*, McFarland & Company, Inc., Jefferson, NC (2010)

(39) Roger L. Kemp, *Documents of American Democracy: A Collection of Essential Works*, McFarland & Company, Inc., Jefferson, NC (2010)

(40) Roger L. Kemp, *Strategies and Technologies for a Sustainable Future*, World Future Society, Bethesda, MD (2010)

(41) Roger L. Kemp, *Cities Going Green: A Handbook of Best Practices*, McFarland & Company, Inc., Jefferson, NC (2011)

(42) Roger L. Kemp, *The Municipal Budget Crunch: A Handbook for Professionals*, McFarland & Company, Inc., Jefferson, NC (2012)

(43) Roger L. Kemp, Frank B. Connolly, and Philip K. Schenck, *Local Government in Connecticut*, 3rd Edition, Wesleyan University Press, Middletown, CT (2013)

(44) Roger L. Kemp, *Town and Gown Relations: A Handbook of Best Practices*, McFarland & Company, Inc., Jefferson, NC (2013)

(45) Roger L. Kemp, *Global Models of Urban Planning: Best Practices Outside the United States*, McFarland & Company, Inc., Jefferson, NC (2013)

(46) Roger L. Kemp, *Urban Transportation Innovations Worldwide: A Handbook of Best Practices Outside the United States*, McFarland & Company, Inc., Jefferson, NC (2015)

(47) Roger L. Kemp, *Immigration and America's Cities: A Handbook on Evolving Services*, McFarland & Company, Inc., Jefferson, NC (2016)

(48) Roger L. Kemp, *Corruption and American Cities: Essays and Case Studies in Ethical Accountability*, McFarland & Company, Jefferson, NC (2016)

(49) Roger L. Kemp, *Privatization in Practice: Reports on Trends, Cases and Debates in Public Service by Business and Nonprofits*, McFarland & Company, Inc., Jefferson, NC (2016)

(50) Roger L. Kemp, *Small Town Economic Development: Reports on Growth Strategies in Practice*, McFarland & Company, Inc., Jefferson, NC (2017)

(51) Roger L. Kemp, Donald F. Norris, Laura Mateczun, Cory Fleming, and Will Fricke, *Cybersecurity: Protecting Local Government Digital Resources*, International City/County Management Association, Washington, D.C. (2017)

(52) Roger L. Kemp, *Eminent Domain and Economic Growth: Perspectives on Benefits, Harms and Trends*, McFarland & Company, Inc., Jefferson, NC (2018)

(53) Roger L. Kemp, *Senior Care and Services: Essays and Case Studies on Practices, Innovations and Challenges*, McFarland & Company, Inc., Jefferson, NC (2019)

(54) Roger L. Kemp, *Cybersecurity: Current Writings on Threats and Protection*, McFarland & Company, Inc., Jefferson, NC (2019)

(55) Roger L. Kemp, *Veteran Care and Services: Essays and Case Studies on Practices, Innovations and Challenges*, McFarland & Company, Inc., Jefferson, NC (2020)

(56) Roger L. Kemp, *Civics 101 – Poems About America's Cities*, Kindle Direct Publishing, Middletown, DE (2020)

(57) Roger L. Kemp, *Civics 102 – Stories About America's Cities*, Kindle Direct Publishing, Middletown, DE (2121)

(58) Roger L. Kemp, *Civics 103 – Charters that Form America's Governments*, Kindle Direct Publishing, Middletown, DE (2121)

(59) Roger L. Kemp, *Civics 104 – America's Evolving Boundaries*, Kindle Direct Publishing, Middletown, DE (2121)

(60) Roger L. Kemp, *Civics 105 – Documents that Formed America*, Kindle Direct Publishing, Middletown, DE (2021)

(61) Roger L. Kemp, *Civics 106 – Documents that Formed the United Kingdom and the United Setates*, Kindle Direct Publishing, Middletown, DE (2021)

H. World Travels by Roge L. Kemp

Roger has visited the following countries, and major geographic regions, throughout the world during his public service and consulting career:

- Australia[14]*
- Austria
- Belgium
- Brunei Darussalam
- Canada
- China

- Czech Republic
- Fiji
- France*
- French Polynesia*
- Germany*
- Hong Kong*
- Hungary
- Iceland
- Indonesia*
- Italy*
- Japan*
- Luxembourg*
- Macau
- Malaysia*
- Mexico
- Netherlands
- New Zealand*
- Philippines*
- Puerto Rico*
- Singapore*

- Slovak Republic
- South Korea*
- Switzerland
- Tahiti*

---

[14] * During his visits to many of these locations, Dr. Kemp has met with elected officials, such as a city's Mayor, administrative officers, and department managers. He has also given presentations at several international professional conferences in some of these nations.

- Thailand
- United Kingdom*
- United States (all regions, and most states)*
- Virgin Islands

I. Some Final Thoughts

Thoughts About America's Cities

El Condor Pasa (If I Could)

I'd rather be a forest than a street.
Yes I would, If I could, I surely would.

I'd rather feel the earth beneath my feet.
Yes I would, If I only could, I surely would.

Simon and Garfunkel, 1970

- - -

America's Livable Cities

Our cities were not designed by city planners,
but by cars, to make the vehicle roadways
and parking spaces available for them.

Our cities must be redesigned by city planners,
to enhance the level of nature within them,
for everyone, especially the citizens who live in our cities.

Roger L. Kemp, 2020

INDEX

Printed in the United States
by Baker & Taylor Publisher Services